From Carp To Dragon

7 Strategies to Awaken, Cultivate and Transform the Dragon in You

Larry Johanson

From Carp To Dragon

Copyright © 2013 by Larry Johanson

All rights reserved. No part of this book may be reproduced or transmitted in any form or by any means without written permission of the author.

ISBN 978-0-9917317-2-5

Dedication

For all those who seek a Path to their dreams and are willing to work to realize them.

Table of Contents

Dedication i
Acknowledgements v
Introduction vii
Strategy #1. Lay A Foundation of Right Character 1
Strategy #2. Cultivate the Dragon's Mindset 29
Strategy #3. Find Your Mission and Purpose 55
Strategy #4. Manage and Invest Your Time Wisely 71
Strategy #5. Breathe Your Stress Away 91
Strategy #6. Develop Effective Communication Skills 115
Strategy #7. Develop Entrepreneurial Skills 147
Conclusion 163
Sources 167
About the Author 169

Acknowledgements

Many people, living and dead, have contributed to the person I've become and I'm enormously grateful to all of them.

Thanks to my mom and dad who because of their treatment forced me to look within and started me on the journey to find meaning and purpose in life.

To Grandma Rosa, whom I never met, but who left a legacy of good deeds that changed the trajectory of my life.

To Aunt Ivy who remembered Grandma Rosa's kindness and repaid it by helping me when I was in desperate straits.

To my beloved sister Myrna, who taught me the value of unconditional love and keeping promises.

To uncle John who brought home a treasure trove of books that opened my mind to undreamt of possibilities.

To the teachers at Wolmer's Boys' School, especially to Mr. Basil McFarlane, who were relentless in instilling the habit of striving for excellence.

To the late Venerable Roshi Philip Kapleau who wordlessly demonstrated that it was possible to awaken to one's True Nature and live with unassailable serenity and peace.

To my present Dharma teacher, Roshi Sunyana Graef whose compassion and example continues to light the Way for me.

To my wife Sonia who continues to be solid as a rock in her support.

To Sean and Matthew who in their own way have taught me salutary lessons in the joys and frustrations of fatherhood and helped me to be a more understanding and forgiving person.

To Ikael Tafari, my Sociology tutor and 'Idren' at the University of the West Indies, who passed too soon, and who opened my eyes to the esoteric dimensions of Rastafari and encouraged me to question the very foundation and assumptions of colonial society.

To the bretheren I hung out with on Brentford Road who taught me the value of One Love, One Heart.

Finally to the amazing community of Zen practitioners, my dharma brothers and sisters in the Triple Sangha, who inspire me through their commitment to the Way, and especially to Joan and Katia, whose artistic and editorial skills improved the quality of this offering.

Introduction

The title of this book *From Carp To Dragon* is inspired by the story in Chinese mythology of the carp that became a dragon. The story goes that carp would swim upstream the Yellow River to spawn. Standing in their way was a waterfall called the Dragon's Gate and only the carp who could leap high enough to get over the fall would pass on upstream. If it leaped high enough, miraculously it would be transformed into a dragon. The dragon in Chinese mythology is a creature of heaven, unlimited and unbounded by time and space. It has the power to control the weather and its passage across the sky is accompanied by thunder, lightning and rain. The dragon also represents immortality, prosperity, good fortune and the imperial authority of the emperors.

My own point of reference for Dragon's Gate, as a Canadian, would be Niagara Falls. Imagine what it would be like for a carp to swim against the current and leap up and over Niagara Falls! To accomplish such a feat would require stupendous courage, discipline, determination and energy.

I first encountered the image of the carp leaping up the waterfall to become a dragon when I took up the practice of Zen meditation in my youth in an effort to deal with the anxiety and stress I felt as a result of the challenges and difficulties I encountered. The purpose of Zen meditation is to come to enlightenment—a state of grace out of which love, joy, compassion and equanimity grows. Needless to say, to arrive at such a state requires the courage, discipline, determination and energy referred to earlier.

Beginning Zen students are likened to the carp that leaps up the waterfall in the attempt to become a dragon. To become a dragon in Zen parlance is to become enlightened. Here, I'm applying the metaphor of transforming from a carp to a dragon to becoming the most awesome, noble, magnificent person you can be; someone who is a high achiever, performing at the top of your game. Such a person would be described as Self-Actualized according to Abraham Maslow. Throughout the book I use the term 'dragon' and achiever interchangeably.

This book is the evolution and culmination of the quest to find answers to the questions of how to be the best I could be and achieve success in life. I began asking myself these questions as a teen. I became obsessed with these questions because of the context I found myself in and the need and desire to escape it. You see, I was born in Jamaica in very humble, you might even say poor circumstances, and grew up in my formative years on a gritty street in Kingston, Jamaica, called Brentford Road. Brentford Road was surrounded on all sides by marginalized ghetto communities—Concrete Jungle to the southwest, Jones Town to the south, and Slipe Road to the east. The streets were ruled by rude boys; guys who carried guns and knives; who hustled, fought against rival rude boy gangs and didn't hesitate to "drop you" (kill you) or "cut you out of your clothes" if you crossed them.

Brentford Road[1] was a magnet for these guys because it was where Studio One, the recording studio of the legendary Clement (Coxone) Dodd was located. Many of the legends on the Jamaican musical scene, people such as Bob Marley, Jacob "Killa" Miller, Dennis Brown, Delroy Wilson, Ken Boothe, to name a few, recorded with

---

[1] Brentford Road is now known as Studio One Boulevard to honour the contribution to Jamaican culture by the Founder and CEO, Clement "Coxsone" Dodd.

Coxone, and it was customary to run into them or other up and coming musicians anxious to find fame and fortune.

My grand aunt, a renowned teacher in her day, had established a preparatory school on Brentford Road, long before the neighborhood became as gritty as it did, and there she stayed until her death. My father, an only child, whose mother died in child birth, was adopted by my grand aunt and for most of his life lived and raised two tribes of his children in this ancestral home. My grand aunt and father died within months of each other and this had a devastating impact on me and my brother and sister. My father died a virtually penniless alcoholic which resulted in the breakup of the family. I could have easily fallen in with the boys on the road but my father's death brought home the realization that I was on my own and if I was going to make something of myself, in spite of the bleak prospects I was faced with, I would have to become focused and disciplined and single minded in my efforts.

What could I do to raise myself out of the dire circumstances I found myself in? Luckily for me, four years before my father died I won a scholarship to Wolmer's Boys', one of the top grammar schools in the country which encouraged academic excellence and cultivating the manners and sensibilities of a gentleman, like its counterparts Harrow and Eaton in England. The year following my father's death I buckled down and hit the books and to my surprise and the surprise of my teachers I rocketed from the bottom of the class to first place. That confirmed for me that I had some potential and for the rest of my time at Wolmer's I hovered at or near the top ten in my class. More importantly, I discovered books, the world of ideas and mentors such a Shakespeare, Socrates, Freud, Jung, Eric Berne, Malcolm X, Karl Marx, Gandhi and a host of others.

The focus and discipline I developed along with the help and support of my extended family gave me the opportunity to finish high school and eventually go to the University of the West Indies where I gained my B.A. degree and then to the University of Windsor, in Canada, where I completed my Master's degree in Communication Studies.

Today, I am an author, speaker, corporate trainer and coach on personal development, leadership and communication issues. I've led seminars in Australia, Britain, Canada and the United States and helped thousands of individuals to become more effective in their lives. I'm also a husband and father.

The chances of me accomplishing what I've achieved, given the context and background from which I came, were very slim. Some of the guys I grew up with on Brentford Road went to prison, or were killed in street fights, or sank into the miasma of the permanent underclass and continued the dubious legacy for themselves and their children of being a "sufferer", the adjective the poor and dispossessed in Jamaica use to describe their chronically hopeless condition.

Part of my process of giving back is sharing what I did to achieve the success that I have. The tools and processes I will be sharing have been tried and tested in the crucible of my own experience. Some have been taken from the experience of others who became my role models and mentors and the books I read.

While no one can guarantee success in life, everyone can give themselves a fighting chance to achieve their dreams if they invest a little time and energy in themselves and are consistent in the application of the principles I am about to share. Notice in the subtitle of the book the first letter of the words "Awaken", "Cultivate" and "Transform" spell the word **ACT**. The best way to benefit from this book is to *take action*. At the end of each strategy I have some Reflection/Action

Steps that I invite you to take based on the content. Do the exercises, jot your responses in the Journal that accompanies this system and take action. To read the book and then put it aside without acting on the principles discussed is a waste of your own time and energy—resources which are too precious to waste.

Identifying the Dragon in You

You may be reading this and wondering if the dragon in you really exists. Until you realize it, the dragon in you remains the vast area of unrealized potential that we're all born with. You could not realize it if it was not hard-wired into your DNA and a latent aspect of yourself. You had early hints of it as a baby when you were driven to take the first faltering steps in spite of the fact that during the first attempts you fell repeatedly until you got the hang of it, realized triumphantly that you could do it, and ran with a new found sense of power and freedom to your proud parents beckoning you from across the room to come to them.

Later as a teen, it expressed itself as the rambunctious, rebellious person bent on exploring the unknown, especially those boundaries and taboos that were imposed on you either by circumstances or tradition.

If you ever climbed a tree that was too tall, jumped off a high cliff or bridge into deep water where you didn't know what the outcome would be, climbed over a fence to retrieve a ball from a yard with a "Beware Dog" sign or did something you were forbidden to do and felt the fear, adrenaline rush and the sense of triumph after you came out of the experience, that was the impulse of the dragon in you. The dragon in you dreams, imagines, wonders "what if?" and asks "why not?" The point here is that the impulse or desire to realize the dragon in you is inborn and natural.

The tragedy for most of us is that we fall asleep, get lazy, go into default mode and succumb to the forces of gravity. Gravity can pull you way down into a pit of mediocrity and failure. Some of us have never quite figured out how to get out of the pool at the bottom of the waterfall and leap over it, past the rainbow and beyond, to realize our dreams. That is why I wrote this book. It is the book that I would have wanted to read when I set out, groping in the dark, to find a path out of the dire straits my father died and left the family in without any real prospects of advancement.

It maps a path to living a life of meaning and purpose, uprightness and productivity; of connection and intimacy with the highest and best in yourself. It is good for young people in high school, for those entering college or university, or leaving university and embarking on their careers. It is good for parents themselves who want to become the best role models for their children. It is good for people who are grappling with change and crisis in their lives—who need to recalibrate their direction in life and re-invent themselves. It is also good for people in the midst of the full catastrophe of their lives who are looking for a process that will help them find peace and freedom.

I've been through all of these stages and in the process have garnered some experience and wisdom. The strategies and the tools, tips, techniques and processes that I share, for the most part, aren't taught in schools or universities. They are distillations of wisdom, knowledge and understanding that come from my experience and the experience of the mentors I embraced. If you would like to awaken the dragon in you, cultivate and transform it so that you realize your potential for greatness by design rather than by luck or chance or default, and in the process save yourself lots of frustration, time, energy and money, then welcome aboard.

You will learn how to lay the foundation for greatness; create the mindset that is invincible and impervious to failure; live with passion and purpose; set and accomplish worthwhile and desirable goals; maintain a vigorous and sustained effort over time, even in the face of seemingly insurmountable odds; deal with stress with equanimity and monetize your gifts and talents.

My unconditional guarantee is that if you apply the principles and processes and take action, at the end of this journey you will know how to harness the power of the dragon in you and let it take you to the pinnacle of your dreams.

This is your journey of personal development and discovery. Let's begin.

STRATEGY #1. LAY A FOUNDATION OF RIGHT CHARACTER

"Right character is the only foundation on which to build true greatness." Larry Johanson

In high school my favourite teacher was Mr. Basil McFarlane who taught English Literature, my favourite subject. Mr. McFarlane exposed us to the works of great authors such as William Shakespeare, George Bernard Shaw, Francis Bacon, Oscar Wilde, and many more. In the works of these authors we came across heroes and villains, examined their motivations and actions, and the consequences of their actions.

As we soared with the triumphs of the heroes and pitied the villains for the tragedies they brought on themselves and those associated with them, it became increasingly clear that what accounted for the successes and failures of these individuals was their character.

Mr. McFarlane would sweep the classroom with his gaze and in a voice that conveyed grave warning would say, "I tell you fellows, show me your character and I'll show you your destiny!" This direct relationship between character and destiny was further reinforced when I began to explore the philosophy and teachings of other religious and philosophical systems outside of Christianity where the familiar and recurring theme in the Bible is that we reap what we sow and what we sow depends on our character.

The Buddha in one of his discourses not only drew a direct relationship between character and destiny but went even further to show how character is formed when he said,

"Sow a thought, reap an act
 Sow an act, reap a habit
 Sow a habit, reap a character
 Sow a character, reap a destiny."

The relationship between character and destiny intrigued me. I reasoned that if character has such a powerful and direct influence on the course and outcome of one's life then it is obviously something that is very important and I had to get some of it. The question is what is it anyway? And how could I go about acquiring it? Is it something we are born with or is it something we can cultivate in the same way that one can grow and cultivate a garden?

Definition of Character

The Collins English Dictionary defines character as:

"The combination of traits and qualities distinguishing the individual nature of a person or thing; moral force or integrity."

[2]John Havercroft and Jan Kielven, define character as, *"a set of beliefs, dispositions or habits of thinking, feeling and acting that make us who we are."*

They note that when an individual's disposition or habits are constructive such a person is regarded as wise or of good character, that no one attribute alone creates character. According to them, it is the growth in understanding, the depth of the collective attributes and the consistent application of these attributes into our daily lives, which creates our character.

The simplest and perhaps the best definition of character I've heard however, is, *"who you are and what you do when no one is watching."* In the lyrics of one of his songs titled, *"Who the Cap Fit"* Bob Marley sings "...and if the night should turn to day, a lot of people would run away, so who the cap fit (sic) let them wear it." Here he is referring to people who do bad things in the dark and would have to run away in the glare of daylight if found out.

Many who engage in unethical behaviour do so because they believe that they won't be caught, so a good rule of thumb for anyone who is about to yield to temptation is to ask themselves, "Can this act or activity stand in the light of day? What if I get caught, what will be the consequences for me, my family, my community?"

Traits of a Person of Right Character

When we say that an individual is a man or woman of character we usually mean that that person is an outstanding individual with

---

[2] Co-authors of an article on Character in the 2003 edition of ***Orbit*** magazine, (Vol. 33, No. 2).

desirable traits. The following traits are universally accepted as traits of a person of right character:

- Courage
- Honesty
- Integrity
- Empathy/Compassion
- Respect
- Responsibility
- Fairness
- Initiative
- Perseverance
- Optimism

Let's take a look at each of these traits and their definitions.

- Courage—facing challenges directly. Doing the right thing even when it may be unpopular. Recognizing risks and dangers and matching our actions to the requirements of the situation.
- Honesty—to be sincere, truthful and trustworthy in our behaviour.
- Integrity—being consistent with what we say and what we do; matching our beliefs with our behaviour.
- Empathy—to sense and appreciate the feelings and emotions of others; to have the ability to "stand in someone else's shoes", or to see things from someone else's perspective even though you may not agree with them personally. Compassion, whose Latin root means to suffer with, is closely related to empathy.
- Respect—to treat ourselves and others with courtesy, dignity and positive regard. To honour the rights of others. To respect the belongings of others, the environment and the world around us.

- Responsibility—to be accountable for our actions. To follow through on our commitments.
- Fairness—to treat others in the way we would like to be treated, (the golden rule). Being sensitive to the needs of others. Interacting with others without stereotyping, prejudice or discrimination. Standing up for human rights.
- Initiative—acting without being prompted by others. Doing what needs to be done without having to be told to do it. Taking the first step towards the achievement of a goal.
- Perseverance—Sticking to a goal and working hard even in the face of obstacles and challenges until the task or assignment is completed.
- Optimism—maintaining a positive attitude. Looking on the brighter side. Seeing the glass as half full instead of being half empty. Identifying opportunities in the face of adversity.

Another way to remember the traits associated with a person of right character is to take the word itself and let each letter that makes up the word stand for a desirable character trait. For example,

Courage; commitment to being the best you can be
Honesty
Achievement oriented
Respect for yourself and others
Attitude—positive, optimistic, 'can do'
Confidence in yourself; compassion and caring for others
Truthful or trustworthy
Excellence
Responsible

> **Action Steps**
>
> 1. Name the people in your life who exhibit the abovementioned traits in their behaviour.
> 2. Which traits are they particularly strong in and how do they exhibit these traits?
> 3. Which traits are you particularly strong in?
> 4. Which traits do you need to work on in order to make them part of your character?

The Difference between a Person of Right Character and a Person of Wrong Character

In our definition and discussion of character please note that the emphasis is on right character. Men and women of right or good character have been in short supply from ancient times. It is said that Diogenes, the ancient Greek philosopher, would walk the streets of Athens in broad daylight with a lamp looking for an honest man. As in the time of Diogenes, the need to find men and women of right character, is just as urgent, perhaps more so than it has ever been. Why?

On almost a daily basis we hear of prominent individuals—CEOs and executives of powerful companies, celebrities and world famous athletes, and politicians, who lie, steal, and cheat to get to the top or to gain unfair advantages. Even ministers of the gospel are frequently reported as engaging in unethical behaviour.

The consequence for all of us is that we lose faith in living lives of virtue, honesty and goodness because we are tempted to say, "of what use is honest, hard work, if others are cheating, lying and stealing and getting away with it?" The temptation is to default to the "dark side" when it appears that no one is watching. Many who have made it to the top have yielded to this temptation and have been disgraced or sent to prison.

It seems that without right character we can get ourselves in a lot of trouble and ruin our lives.

Examples of men and women who have fallen spectacularly from the pinnacles of their society because of flaws in their character abound in Literature and in life. An example in Literature is Macbeth, the character in Shakespeare's play of the same name. Naked ambition and the lust for power led him to be seduced by witches and his wife into committing murder for the throne of Scotland. That act eventually led to his and his wife's death and a great deal of suffering for the people affected by their actions.

In real life there is the example of Bernie Madoff, the financier, whose $65 billion fraud, threatened the foundations of institutions and sent 70 year old pensioners back to work because they lost everything they invested with him. His son, Mark Madoff, committed suicide, because of the shame and his own presumed guilt in the fraud.

Here in Canada we have the case of Conrad Black, the Canadian newspaper baron, who was convicted of corporate fraud in a U.S. court and sentenced to six and a half years in jail.

In the sports arena we have the examples of Ben Johnson the Canadian 100 metre sprinter who won gold in the 1988 Olympics in Seoul, South Korea, with a world record of 9.79 seconds and American Olympic champion, Marion Jones who won three gold and two bronze medals in the 2000 Sydney Olympics. Both were disqualified for using drugs and Jones served time in prison for lying to a grand jury about her drug use.

And recently, Lance Armstrong, the seven time tour de France bicycle champion, was stripped of all his titles because he was accused of, and subsequently admitted to doping. These are just a few examples. Over the last few years, more and more scandals have surfaced of CEOs, politicians, lawyers, doctors, ministers of the gospel, Olympic athletes, and even an astronaut, who have behaved in ways that are below the expectations of society for people with the intelligence, influence, power and prestige these individuals possessed.

All the individuals, and the categories of individuals we mentioned, were men and women who by the standard measures of achievement were great achievers. They had ambition, discipline, drive, energy, which gave them the competitive edge and allowed them to achieve great success, but they also had fatal flaws in their character. They had cracks in their ethical and moral foundation and we all know that any structure built on a weak foundation will eventually collapse.

As is the case of constructing a building on a weak foundation, which ultimately collapses, so is the case if your achievement is built on blind ambition, naked self interest, dishonesty and deception. But if your achievement is built on the rock solid foundation of right or good character, it will stand no matter how hard the winds and storms of temptation and adversity blow against it.

The Price People of Wrong Character Pay

The price people of wrong or flawed character pay is not only the loss of their wealth, their power or their prestige. The most telling loss is the loss of their reputations. It is possible to regain wealth and power, but it is almost impossible to recover a reputation that is tarnished, especially when you have been tried and found guilty in a court of law, in public opinion or by your peers. Why is it so difficult to recover a tarnished reputation?

It takes many years, often a lifetime, to build the trust and the social capital that goes into building a reputation. Your reputation is the result of how the society and your social group see you. How you are perceived is based on your actions. People don't like to be duped and they exact a high price to buy back the trust they placed in you. There will always be someone out there who may not be as willing as others to forgive and forget that you broke a law or committed a crime, especially if such a crime caused great suffering for many people. That person may be a major obstruction to the opening of any other doors of opportunity for you.

Someone who commits fraud, for example, cannot hope to get a job in a bank or be employed in a position where he is trusted with money. And if that person is in a situation where money is stolen, he becomes the first suspect. Shakespeare's Othello says, "Who steals my purse, steals trash…but he that filches from me my good name, makes me poor indeed."

Universal Codes of Conduct for People of Right Character

What gives people of right character a huge competitive advantage over people of wrong or flawed character are the universal codes of conduct that they live by. These codes of conduct are common principles that all the world's great religions and wisdom traditions recommend that we should live by. They all assert that there is a Higher Power, whatever name we call it, depending on our cultural backgrounds and belief systems.

These religious and wisdom traditions assert that we are connected to each other through this Higher Power which is greater and larger than our individual selves. To live in accordance with our Higher Power requires that we respect and live by the following codes of conduct: [3]

1. **Not to kill our fellow human beings but to regard their lives as equally precious as ours and to love them as we love ourselves.** By extension we are encouraged to see the earth itself as a living entity and to protect it. This is the basis of the Environmental or Green Movement and we're realizing that if we harm the earth, we harm ourselves.

2. **Not to steal but to respect the property of others.** One of the things I am most proud of during my youth was turning in a huge sum of money I found in the bathroom of my high school. I later learned that it was money for books and tuition which fell out of the pocket of one of my schoolmates. The principal announced in the assembly the next morning what I had done and congratulated me for turning in the money. He said that I was an example of the kind of person the school was interested in turning out into the society.

   The student whose pocket the money fell out of thanked me very much. Turning in this money paid and continues to pay me huge bonuses all these years later in the feelings I have of being a good, honest, trustworthy person and that I should continue to be this kind of person. What would have happened if I had kept the money? If I got away with it I would remember with shame and guilt all these years later that I had stolen the money.

   If I was caught I probably would have been expelled from the school and punished by my parents who would be embar-

---

[3] I am indebted to the Zen tradition, specifically the lineage of Roshi Philip Kapleau, for the framing of these codes of conduct.

rassed by my conduct. Were there schoolmates who thought I was stupid for turning in the money when I could have had a great time spending it? Of course, but having a clear conscience was more valuable to me than the short term satisfaction of what I could have purchased with the money.

3. **Not to lie but to speak the truth and to be honest in our dealings with others**. People who form a habit of lying invariably lose the capacity to distinguish truth from falsehood. Sooner or later their social circles realize that they are untrustworthy and limit contact with them especially after they have been repeatedly caught in the lie.

4. **Not to engage in improper sexuality but to be caring and responsible**. Tiger Woods, Dominique Strauss-Kahn, former Congressman Anthony Wiener, Eliot Spitzer, Arnold Schwarzenegger are recent examples of individuals who fell from grace in the public's eye because they engaged in improper sexual conduct and relations. Their actions had devastating consequences for their careers, their spouses and their families. The three greatest temptations according to Yogananda, the Indian sage who founded the Self Realization Fellowship, are money, sex and drugs.

To be caring and responsible in our sexual relations is to assume responsibility for the spiritual, emotional, and physical well-being of the person with whom you've entered into a sexual relationship. Today, more than ever, it is incumbent on us to exercise restraint in indulging our sexual appetites as AIDS, the sexually transmitted disease that has defined the present age, is capable of devastating whole societies. The bottom line when it comes to sexuality is, "do no harm."

5. **Not to cloud your mind with drugs and alcohol but to maintain clarity and good judgment.** The consequences of taking drugs and alcohol can be devastating for the individual who takes them and the individuals who are impacted by the actions of those who take alcohol and drugs. In Jamaican society, using alcohol and marijuana are deeply embedded in the culture as desirable social and cultural past times. A rite of passage for many young men, and the sign that one had transitioned into adulthood, was to be invited by an older man, in many cases one's father, for a drink. A valued compliment was that one could hold one's liquor, meaning that one could imbibe lots without showing signs of drunkenness.

My own father was an alcoholic who said and did very painful things to me and the rest of his family and was totally oblivious to the hurt that he caused because he was numbed by alcohol. I was alienated from him and had a great deal of resentment which I struggled over many years to overcome.

For many young people, marijuana was the drug of choice especially for those who came under the influence of Rastafarians who saw marijuana as a sacrament of their faith. Unfortunately, there were some who experienced psychotic episodes as a result of smoking marijuana. Many never recovered.

In July 2008, the devastating impact that alcohol and drugs can have on the lives of people was clearly demonstrated to me when a drunk driver lost control of the vehicle he was driving and t-boned me and my son while we were waiting at a stop sign to enter a major roadway. After he rammed us, buckling our car, his major concern was to get away. In his effort to do so he lost control a second time and rammed a tree before getting out and "crab-walking" his way down the road, according to my son. I thought I was only minutes from dying because of the searing pain shooting through my chest and all I could do was watch helplessly as this man staggered off down the road in his effort to get away.

Fortunately, someone who had seen him weaving across the road called the police and followed him to his home where he was arrested. I am fortunate that I and my son escaped devastating physical injury or death, but the trauma of having such a close call lingers for the both of us, especially for my son, who at his age has developed a sobering realization that one's life can be taken away in an instant. It is not a perspective that I would have wanted him to have, as youth is a time to test and push the boundaries of one's life.

So the next time you're tempted to drink alcohol or do drugs, **STOP** and visualize the drink or the drug robbing you of clarity and good judgment, your guardians against doing something that could negatively impact the course of your life and the life of others forever.

6. **Not to speak of the faults of others, but to be understanding and sympathetic**. This and the following code of conduct deal with the importance of right speech. To be critical of others, to gossip and carry news can destroy the harmony of a community. The old saying that "Sticks and stones may break my bones but words cannot hurt me" is only a half-truth. Words certainly cannot hurt one physically in the way sticks and stones can, but they can cause a great deal of emotional and psychological harm. Oftentimes, the pain of an injudicious comment can last a lifetime, long after the hurt from a physical blow has diminished or healed.

7. **Not to praise one's self and put others down, but to work to overcome one's own shortcomings.** Jesus' admonition to take the beam out of one's own eye before taking the mote out of the eye of others speaks to this principle. Focusing on our shortcomings instead of criticizing others keeps us humble and continuously working for our own improvement.

8. **Not to be mean, but to share freely what you have with others; to be generous and kind.** The phrase "it is better to give than to receive" speaks to the good fortune of being in a position to be a giver of charity rather than a receiver of alms and thus to be grateful that you are in a position to be your brother's and sister's keeper. Often the random and capricious wave of Fortune's hand can be enough to destroy the fortress of security that one has built and send one into the ranks of the needy.

9. **Not to indulge in anger, but to exercise control.** Anger is one of the most destructive emotions both for the person who indulges in it and the person to whom it is directed. It has been found that people who are perpetually angry are prone to high blood pressure and heart attacks. Anger opens the gate to hatred and hatred oftentimes leads to war and murder.

10. **Recognize the code as an expression of your Higher Power in action and surrender to it.** This was the advice of one of my mentors who admitted that his character was not strong enough to withstand the temptations he knew he would succumb to if he didn't cling to the code as a man does to a life raft in choppy seas.

It is important to note how interconnected these codes of conduct are. To break one is to run the risk of breaking them all. For example, in the reality TV show *48 Hours,* there was an episode where an individual hooked on drugs decided to steal his colleague's stash and in the process killed him. The breaking of one code led to the breaking of others and the destruction of lives.

A Step By Step Process for Building Right Character

The question then is how can one go about building right character? The Bible is explicit in its advice on building right character when it states in Philippians chapter 4 verse 8:

"Whatever is true, whatever is noble, whatever is pure, whatever is lovely, whatever is admirable—if anything is excellent or praiseworthy, think about such things."

My understanding of the word "think" in this passage is to concentrate on, focus on, meditate on, ponder, inscribe on your heart and mind. You become what you think and focus your thoughts and attention on. James Allen in the powerful essay titled, *"As A Man Thinketh"* asserts that "A man is literally **what he thinks**, his character being the complete sum of all his thoughts." The first step therefore in building right character is to think right thoughts.

Life as a Class Room or Testing Ground

There are many systems of thought that believe that character is built as we face the challenges and obstacles of everyday life. They see life as a class-room or testing ground of challenges and obstacles. No matter who we are, sooner or later as human beings we'll all experience pain, loss and suffering. We 'graduate' by developing our spiritual, mental, emotional and physical strength by taking on these challenges and obstacles and overcoming them. Building character is essentially a choice; how we choose to respond to the difficulties and challenges of our lives.

The Chinese character for danger and opportunity is the same. Right where we encounter a difficulty is an opportunity to use that difficulty to strengthen our resolve and sharpen our spirits. In Zen, there's an expression that says seven times down eight times up! This means that it does not matter how often one stumbles and falls, the most important thing is to get up and keep going.

Calvin Coolidge, the 30th President of the United States said,

"Nothing in the world can take the place of Persistence. Talent will not; nothing is more common than unsuccessful men with talent. Genius will not; unrewarded genius is almost a proverb. Education will not; the world is full of educated derelicts. Persistence and determination alone are omnipotent. The slogan "Press On" has solved and always will solve the problems of the human race."

Men and women of right character respond to the challenges and adversities in their lives with courage; they make Hope their Northern Star—the fixed point on the compass that guides them. They dig deep to find the perseverance, the will, the energy, the vision to keep going, even when they are surrounded by difficulties and the odds of succeeding seem slim; they push on even when others around them are throwing up their hands in despair and surrendering to their difficulties. Building right character is being persistent in the face of adversities, challenges and setbacks.

Building right character is a systematic and deliberate process that you engage in on a daily basis. Here are six more steps you can take to build right character:

1. **Challenge yourself to develop good habits.** Here is a process you can follow:

   ➢ Think of a character trait you would like to develop.
   ➢ Define the trait.
   ➢ Begin a journal about that trait and why you want to develop it.
   ➢ Tell your inner circle of family and friends that you want to develop that trait and ask them to keep you accountable when you fall short. For example, if you are prone to getting angry and you want to develop more self-control, then tell your family and friends that this is what you want to accomplish and enlist their support in helping you develop this trait.
   ➢ Keep track of the circumstances under which you find it most difficult to exhibit that trait and resolve to do better when you lose your cool.
   ➢ It usually takes about 30 days to develop a new habit, so be prepared to work on your new habit for this period of time.
   ➢ Track your progress and reward yourself for your successes.

2. **Seek out people you admire and ask them to mentor you**. The surest way to succeed is to model successful people. For the most part, people who have accomplished much in their lives are willing to share experiences and give advice as one of the ways in which they give back to society. Take them for lunch, offer to volunteer for, or contribute to their favourite charity and they'll probably reward you with priceless information, advice and contacts.

3. **Be friends with people of good character**. The friends you keep can influence you for good or ill. Sometimes people get themselves in trouble by being in the company of friends when a crime

is committed and although they are innocent are judged guilty by association.

4. **Read the biographies of outstanding people,** especially those who remained people of character under very challenging and difficult circumstances and let them inspire you. Abraham Lincoln, Mahatma Gandhi, Martin Luther King Jr. and Nelson Mandela are great examples.

5. **Read the works of great authors**. Ask people whom you admire to recommend books that inspired them.

6. **Expose yourselves to great ideas**. Examples of such ideas are "Democracy"; "Freedom"; "Equality"; "Justice". These are concepts and ideas that countries in Western Europe, Canada and the United States have built their societies on and hold dear. They are things that people have died for in other societies.

An example of someone who transformed his life by applying steps four, five and six was Malcolm X, the African American Muslim minister and human rights activist. In 1998, *Time Magazine* named his autobiography, *The Autobiography of Malcolm X* one of the most influential books in the twentieth century.

Malcolm X had a difficult early life and ended up in prison where he turned his life around through a process of reading and intellectual development. He became a great orator and champion for the rights of African Americans. When he went to prison he was barely literate and unable to write legibly. In an excerpt from his autobiography on how he transformed himself in prison he said,

> "I saw that the best thing that I could do was get hold of a dictionary—to learn some words...I spent two days just riffling uncertainly

through the dictionary's pages. I'd never realized so many words existed!

I didn't know **which** words I needed to learn. Finally just to start some kind of action, I began copying…I copied…everything printed on that first page down to the punctuation marks. I believe it took me a day. Then, aloud I read back to myself everything I had written…

I woke up the next morning, thinking about those words—immensely proud to realize that not only had I written so much at one time, but I had written words that I never knew were in the world.

Moreover, with a little effort, I could also remember what many of these words meant. I reviewed the words whose meanings I didn't remember. I was so fascinated that I went on—I copied the dictionary's next page…With every succeeding page, I also learned of people and places and events from history. Finally, the dictionary's 'A' section had filled a whole tablet—and I went on into the 'B's. That was the way I started copying what eventually became the entire dictionary.

Between what I wrote in my tablet, and writing letters, during the rest of my time in prison I would guess I wrote a million words…" (p.175-6)

In my own case what set me apart early on from the other guys on Brentford Road was the fact that I was a voracious reader. The more I read the more the world of ideas opened up for me as one author would refer to another author who influenced him or her. As my vocabulary increased the sharper my intellect became and very soon I discovered philosophers such as Plato and Socrates, authors such as Somerset Maugham, D H Lawrence, Dostoyevsky, and Tolstoy, and philosophical and religious systems such as Buddhism and Hinduism.

My discovery of Zen Buddhism totally changed my outlook and saved my life.

My intellectual horizon expanded so much that in time I outgrew the guys on the corner. Getting high or getting laid did not interest me as much as the concepts and ideas I encountered in the books I read and I realized that in my imagination I had outgrown the confines of the narrow working class context I had grown up in. I wanted to travel, meet people and explore the concepts and ideas I discovered. The outcome was that the critical mass of ideas and thoughts I encountered in the books I read eventually led me to go to university. Of all the boys I grew up with on Brentford Road, the only one I know of who went to university was me.

The harder I worked, the "luckier" I became and in time other opportunities opened up which eventually took me to Canada, where I now live, and since then to Australia, Britain, across Canada and the U.S. doing seminars on personal development, and to Japan and China on pilgrimages in pursuit of my interest in Zen Buddhism.

In order to escape the context of poverty and difficult social conditions I found myself in, I had to resolve to do so and impose a ruthless discipline on myself. At every juncture where I transitioned from one stage to the next I had to summon up greater courage to take the leap, often without knowing fully how things would turn out.

Many times I found myself standing literally on the edge of the precipice trembling in terror as I contemplated stepping from my known world into the unknown and doing so in spite of my fear and trembling. Having lived through great adversity, I can say for sure that we're all stronger than what we think we are, and are capable of transforming ourselves from carps into dragons if we really have the desire and the will to soar to summits we only dared to dream of at one time or the other.

The response of the carp to the call to greatness is to leap. For it to leap over the waterfall it has to summon up everything in itself that is powerful and noble. And it takes more than one leap. The leap is a continuous process of practice—minute by minute, hour by hour, day by day, month by month, year by year, decades by decades. In the process of its continuing practice it builds willpower, vigour, energy, muscles, know-how, confidence and mindset.

These very qualities cause it to leap higher and higher and one day in a graceful and mighty but paradoxically effortless leap, it finds itself sailing higher and higher, gathering momentum until it finds itself in a graceful arc vaulting over the waterfall. In that instant the dragon emerges in all its awesome lightning and thunder form, powerful and unstoppable.

The message here is that there is hope for everyone no matter where they are. We are only defeated when we give up on ourselves. We can turn our lives around if we have the vision, the courage, and the determination, and engage the help and support of able helpers. But the bottom line is that building the right character requires **YOUR OWN EFFORTS**. No one can do it for you.

Benjamin Franklin's Process for Building Right Character

The process which I outlined in the first of the six steps above is remarkably similar to the process Benjamin Franklin embarked on when he "conceived the bold and arduous task of arriving at moral perfection" in his youth. Benjamin Franklin was one of the Founding Fathers of the United States. He was a noted printer, author, scientist, inventor, musician, statesman and diplomat and made many significant contributions to a wide spectrum of American life. In today's term he could be called a "Renaissance man", that is someone who is well educated or who excels in a wide variety of subjects or fields.

His process of building right character was introduced by my Zen teacher during the annual term students program where members of our community pledge to work more intensely on their practice and integrate it in their daily lives over the course of eight weeks. This may include community work, setting aside more time for meditation, and paying greater attention to keeping the precepts. My teacher thought that Franklin's method would help us to integrate the precepts more effectively in our daily lives.

Here is what Benjamin Franklin[4] did. First he decided on the virtues he wanted to cultivate and defined them. The virtues with his definitions were:

i. **Temperance**. Eat not to dullness, drink not to elevation.
ii. **Silence**. Speak not but what may benefit others or yourself; avoid trifling conversations.
iii. **Order**. Let all your things have their places; let each part of your business have its time.
iv. **Resolution**. Resolve to perform what you ought; perform without fail what you resolve.
v. **Frugality**. Make no expense but to do good to others or yourself; i.e. waste nothing.
vi. **Industry**. Lose no time; be always employed in something useful; cut off all unnecessary actions.
vii. **Sincerity**. Use no hurtful deceit; think innocently and justly, and, if you speak, speak accordingly.
viii. **Justice**. Wrong none by doing injuries, or omitting the benefits that are your duty.
ix. **Moderation**. Avoid extremes; forbear resenting injuries so much as you think they deserve.
x. **Cleanliness**. Tolerate no uncleanliness in body, clothes, or habitation.

---

[4] The Autobiography of Benjamin Franklin, Houghton Mifflin Company, 1923.

xi. **Tranquility**. Be not disturbed at trifles, or at accidents common or unavoidable.
xii. **Chastity**. Rarely use venery but for health or offspring, never to dullness, weakness, or the injury of your own or another's peace or reputation.
xiii. **Humility**. Imitate Jesus and Socrates. (p. 122-123)

He then made a "little book" to which he allotted a page for each of the virtues. He drew a table for each page with 7 columns (one for each day of the week) and 13 rows for each of the 13 virtues he wished to develop. He then focused his attention on that virtue each day for a week with the object to "mark by a little black spot, every fault I found upon examination to have been committed respecting that virtue upon that day." (p.125)

His process involved paying strict attention to each of the virtues successively over the course of a week with the goal in respect of the virtue he focused on to keep each line clear of spots. Thus for the first week he would focus on *Temperance*. Whether he gave himself a black spot or not regarding a particular virtue depended on a rigorous process of self reflection at the end of the day. He would then move on to the next virtue for the following week with the intention to keep both lines clear and so on.

Form of the pages

Virtues	Temperance						
	Eat not to dullness; Drink not to elevation						
	S	M	T	W	T	F	S
T.							
S.	*	*		*		*	
O.	* *	*	*		*	*	*
R.			*			*	
F.		*			*		
I.			*				
S.							
J.							
M.							
C.							
T.							
C.							
H.							

This process took thirteen weeks which he repeated four times in the course of a year.

"And like him who, having a garden to weed, does not attempt to eradicate all the bad herbs at once, which would exceed his reach and his strength, but works on one of the beds at a time, and, accomplished the first, proceeds to a second, so I should have, I hoped, the encouraging pleasure of seeing on my pages the progress I made in virtue, by clearing successively my lines of their spots, till in the end, by a number of courses, I should be happy in viewing a clean book, after thirteen weeks' daily examination." (p.125)

This is as brilliant, systematic and thorough a system one could devise to build right character as I've seen and I heartily recommend it.

The Impact and Influence of Men and Women of Right Character

Not only do men and women of right character have a competitive advantage over others, they also have impact and influence far beyond their own lives, time and society. They become beacons of light, hope and inspiration for others and affirm our belief in humanity. That is perhaps the greatest legacy one can leave behind. The following are examples of such men and women, who, through the force of their character became beacons of light and symbols of courage and hope for all of us.

Mahatma Gandhi

Mahatma Gandhi loosened the powerful grip of the British Empire on his country and people through civil disobedience and the moral force of non-violent protest.

Rosa Parks

Rosa Parks was an ordinary black woman, who sparked the Civil Rights movement in the United States by refusing, with quiet grace and dignity, to sit at the back of the bus anymore, but to exercise her right as a citizen of the United States to be treated with fairness and equality.

Nelson Mandela

Nelson Mandela, the father of a free South Africa, whose steely determination, and vision of justice and equality, brought the perpetrators of apartheid to the negotiation table, and when he won them to his view, avoided a bloodbath by offering forgiveness and reconciliation.

Mother Teresa

Mother Teresa devoted her life to bringing healing and comfort to the poor people in the slums of Calcutta.

Martin Luther King Junior

Martin Luther King Junior, a hero of the Civil Rights movement in the Unites States, who refused to fight hate with hate, but committed himself and his followers to non-violence, and declared to America his dream that all people, regardless of their color, race, and creed could live together in harmony.

Terry Fox

Terry Fox, our own Canadian hero, who instead of feeling sorry for himself and retreating into a corner after he lost his leg to cancer, ran on one leg and brought the whole world to its feet to run and walk for a cure for cancer.

Barack Obama

Barack Obama, the first black president of the United States, who dared to believe that he, could achieve something that no other black or white person believed he could, and sold his fellow Americans the notion that "Yes we can!"

It is said that coal becomes diamond under intense heat and pressure. These men and women of right character, like coal, became diamonds under the intense heat and pressure of the circumstances they found themselves in. They made the transformational leap from being ordinary human beings to become extraordinary **human beams** in situations where others would have buckled under the pressure.

They shine with the greatness that is inherent in all of us and they are the kinds of examples we can follow. As part of your own process of building right character I recommend that you read their biographies, autobiographies, philosophies and ideas and implement what resonates with you in your life.

Our Birthright

I believe that all of us as human beings are born with the natural impulse to do good; to be good; and to be the best we can be. This impulse becomes our conscience and we naturally seem to know when we're not honouring or living up to it. We feel badly when we hurt ourselves or others; when we lie, cheat or steal even when no one knows what we have done. I am of course referring to 'normal' people.

We know that there are people, sociopaths and psychopaths, who completely lack the empathy and compassion of ordinary people and are capable of great cruelty. The horror with which we respond to the behaviour of such people tells us how far outside the norm they have fallen.

We don't need parents, teachers, priests, judges or the police to tell us when we've done wrong. All we have to do is pay attention to the still, small voice of our conscience. People who find themselves in trouble muffle their consciences and as a consequence, lose the compass that points them in the right direction. They end up hurting themselves and others and fall short of realizing their potential.

You will know that you have become a person of right character when you honour the impulse to be good and do the right thing, regardless of whether anyone is watching. Men and women of right character make a continuous effort to honour this birthright.

Summary

The key points to remember in laying down a foundation of right character are:

- Character is destiny.
- Right character is the only foundation on which to build true greatness.
- The traits of a person of right character can be developed in a deliberate and systematic way using the strategies outlined and the processes modeled by Benjamin Franklin.
- The universal codes of conduct can be used as the scaffolding to support you as you lay the foundation for building an imposing and magnificent structure of right character.
- Men and women of right character become beacons of light for humanity.
- Your birthright is to become such a person.

In Strategy #2 you'll learn how to Cultivate the Dragon's Mindset.

Strategy #2. Cultivate the Dragon's Mindset

"The Dragon's Mindset is the mindset that in its resolve cuts through all fears and doubts, like the diamond which cuts through everything but cannot be cut by anything. The only word to describe the Dragon's Mindset is "Invincible." Larry Johanson

All great enterprises, which ultimately are calls to greatness, require deep faith in one's self. The carp can only take on the task of leaping over the waterfall because it fully believes in itself. If it swam around at the bottom of the fall bemoaning the fact that it was only a poor little carp, and who was it to think that it could become a dragon, then no dragons would be born. In this strategy we'll explore how to cultivate the mindset of the dragon and the processes involved in developing the right attitudes and beliefs that support us in our efforts to achieve our dreams. In exploring the mindset of the dragon it is perhaps best to define what I mean by the term "mindset."

I use the term "mindset" to refer to the whole superstructure of awareness, attitudes, beliefs, consciousness, and mentality; the habitual thinking processes that shape how we see ourselves in relation to the world, our self-confidence and self-esteem. The dragon's mindset can be described as "no limits" "possibility thinking" that supports us in "boldly going where no one has gone before", to borrow the words of the mission statement of the star ship *Enterprise* in the Star Trek series.

An example of this "no limits" "possibility thinking" was seen when President Kennedy announced and committed the United States in 1961 to the goal of putting a man on the moon and returning him safely to earth before the end of the decade, a feat accomplished on July 20, 1969 when Neil Armstrong, the Apollo 11 Commander, stepped on the lunar surface with the immortal words, "That's one small step for man, one giant leap for mankind."

When Kennedy made the announcement it was a paradigm shattering concept. Had the scientists and astronauts who were engaged in this endeavour questioned their abilities, or expressed doubt in achieving this goal we would probably still be earthbound wondering if it is possible. Today, we're talking about going to Mars or colonizing the moon or building cities in the ocean.

What are Attitudes?

Having the right attitude is a key part of the dragon's mindset. We've often heard the expression "Your attitude determines your altitude." According to Charles Swindoll, attitude is more important than facts. "It is more important than the past, than education, than money, than circumstances, than failures, than successes, than what other people think, or say or do. It is more important than appearance, giftedness, or skill."

 So what are attitudes? Attitudes are the thoughts and feelings we have about ourselves and the world, and the way we communicate these through our behaviour. Attitudes can be right or wrong, positive or negative. The right attitude is one that helps us accomplish our goals and dreams, assuming that those goals and dreams are ethical, legal and moral. How do we determine that someone has the right attitude? What kind of behaviour would they exhibit?

Someone with the right attitude would exhibit the following behaviour:

- Positive
- Energetic
- Cooperative
- Smiling
- Sense of humor
- Happy
- Problem solver; focused on 'can do'

Someone with the wrong attitude would be:

- Negative
- Lethargic
- Uncooperative
- Scowling
- Serious; gloomy
- Depressed
- Whiner; complainer; focused on 'can't'

People with the wrong attitude are invariably what I call "energy vampires." When you are around them you feel tired, or drained. Dr. Eric Berne, creator of Transactional Analysis and author of *What Do You Say After You Say Hello?* noted that there are four basic attitudes. These are:

1. I am o.k. You're o.k.
2. I am o.k. You're not o.k.
3. I am not o.k. You're o.k.

4. I am not o.k. You're not o.k.

These attitudes are accompanied by three types of behaviour, namely, assertive, aggressive and passive behaviour.

Attitudes and Behaviour of Assertive People

- I am o.k. You're o.k.
- Respect themselves and others
- Seek win/win solutions in conflict situations

Attitudes and Behaviour of Aggressive People

- I am o.k. You're not o.k.
- Anger
- Sarcasm
- Blame
- Threats
- Ignore other people's feelings
- Seek win/lose solutions in conflict situations

Attitudes and Behaviour of Passive People

- I am not o.k. You're o.k.
- Victims
- Cooperate with others to hurt them
- Anxious to please
- Stressed and frustrated
- Accept lose/win solutions in conflict situations

Of the four attitudes, the one that is perhaps most difficult to work with is the one that operates from the position of "I am not o.k. You're not o.k." Some of the rude boys I grew up with on Brentford Road operated from that position and we knew instinctively to avoid them because they communicated very clearly that they had nothing to live for and so they could easily in a fight kill someone, die or go to prison. A few of them did go to prison seeing it as a badge of honour that would garner them more credit as bad guys because of the "respect", (read fear) people had of them. The best way to deal with someone who conveys the message that they are not o.k. and you're not o.k. is to avoid them.

Attitudes, Behaviour and Self Esteem

Our attitudes and behaviour are influenced by how we feel about ourselves or our self esteem. In this section we will look at this issue of self esteem, how we come to develop self esteem and what we can do to improve our self esteem.

Psychologists argue that the minds of newborn infants are like blank sheets of paper. They have no concept of a self separate and apart from the world, nor do they have a self concept. They don't know whether they are male or female, rich or poor, black or white. As they grow and develop and begin to interact with the world they begin to learn about themselves, their roles and where they fit in the society. What they learn about themselves shape their self concept. Their self concept shapes their self esteem and their self esteem in turn impacts their self confidence.

To *"esteem"* someone according to the *Collins English Dictionary*, is to have great respect or regard for that person. Self-esteem can thus be defined as the respect, regard or attitude one has for oneself. It defines self-confidence as belief in one's own abilities or self assurance. Self esteem and self confidence can be high or low, positive or negative.

The Development of Self Esteem

During the course of our lives different people and institutions play a significant role in the development of our self esteem. Some of the most important are:

- Parents.
- Teachers.
- Friends.
- Media.
- Religious institutions.

The Impact of Parents

Our parents have the earliest impact on our sense of worthiness. This is communicated in what they said to us, and how they treated us physically. Were they attentive and responsive to our needs? Were they encouraging in the things they said to us as we explored and learned about our world? Or were they critical and communicated their lack of confidence in us to rise to the challenges all of us are destined to face in our lives.

Dr Eric Berne notes that just the setting for one's conception was an important factor in one's life. Did our parents have a loving, respectful and stable relationship? Did they look forward to our conception and birth or did they regard our conception as a mistake? And where were they in their own development as individuals when they became parents? Were they emotionally and financially stable or were they still struggling to find themselves and their way in the world? All of these were factors which impacted how you were treated as a child.

My own struggles with self esteem began with a very difficult relationship with my parents, especially my father, who was both verbally and physically abusive. They also openly showed preferences for their children based on standards of beauty that were part of the colonial heritage of Jamaican society. "Better hair" and more European features were considered more attractive. I had what was described as "coarse" hair and on the spectrum of the mixed Aboriginal, Afro-European heritage of my family I was regarded as more on the African side, and got the message that I wasn't as attractive as my siblings.

In addition, as the eldest, I was saddled with lots of chores while my siblings enjoyed lots of leisure and play time. The injunction to take care of my younger siblings at the expense of my own needs was also imposed on me. The consequence was that I grew up with a combination of 'Cinderfella' (my version of Cinderella) and Ugly Duckling complexes. I spent a long time grappling with these complexes before I finally managed to understand that my parents themselves were a product of their environment and they too suffered from low self esteem. In the same way that they transmitted their physical genes, they also transmitted their unhealthy psychic genes. They would have had to be a lot more self-aware to avoid the pitfall of passing on the toxic legacy of a colonial society that judged itself on the standards set by its British colonial masters.

It took a great deal of education, introspection and self awareness to come to an understanding of the forces, often unconscious, that shaped my parents and me, and a great deal more work to heal the emotional and psychological wounds and sense of unworthiness that haunted me. It was only after realizing how difficult it was to become self-aware, and recognizing the limited intellectual, emotional and spiritual tools my parents possessed, which made it virtually impossible for them to escape the conditioning of their environment, was I able eventually to forgive them and take full responsibility for how I defined and felt about myself. One cannot become a dragon while wallowing in self-pity and victimhood.

Larry Johanson

The Impact of Teachers

Our teachers are the next set of important people in our lives. Many of us can remember a teacher who played a pivotal role in our lives in encouraging and inspiring us to strive for excellence and who became role models. I was fortunate to attend a high school, a rare privilege in Jamaican society, which had a culture of high expectation for its students. We were all expected to go on to university, get a profession and become productive members of society.

Earlier on I mentioned the impact of Mr. Basil McFarlane, my high school English Literature teacher, who modeled passion and energy, and exhorted us to live upright, productive lives. I still draw upon that legacy which he bequeathed to his students and which I in turn offer to my own son and people who attend my seminars. Some people were not as fortunate as me and had teachers who expressed little confidence in their ability to succeed in life, and in some cases predicted failure and ruin. For some, that was the spur to prove their teachers wrong that drove them, and for others, that was a curse that confirmed for them that they didn't have what it took to succeed.

The Impact of Friends

As we grew older and entered our teenage and young adult years our friends played a more important role in our lives than our parents and teachers. They reinforced us in our identities or helped us develop new identities. Were we part of a popular in-group; first among equals or were we outcast, teased, bullied and called names? In high school and on Brentford Road I had a mixed experience of being bullied, teased and called names and floated on the fringes of the in group. In time I developed a *modus operandi* of staying connected while at the same time pursuing my own path.

The Impact of Media

As we engaged the wider society and started to consume popular culture through the mass and social media we began to be aware of images, popular beliefs and stereotypes about our cultural groups, socio-economic backgrounds, gender, sexual orientation and on the basis of what we picked up, began to form opinions about ourselves and others. Where did we fit in our society? Were we o.k. or not o.k.? Were people like us portrayed positively or negatively? Did we see positive role models, people that looked like us with the same backgrounds in the media?

The Impact of Religious Institutions

Our religious institutions also played a significant role in our concept of ourselves. I grew up in a fundamentalist Christian context which shaped my early notions of the nature of man, the character of women, temptation, the devil and sex based on the story of Adam and Eve. These are concepts and ideas that one has to grapple with as one develops a philosophy grounded in reality and reason. What did you learn from your tradition about the nature of man and the character of women? And what did you learn about God? Was He a jealous, vengeance seeking old guy or was She a loving and compassionate mother? And what were you taught about other people who practiced religious and sacred paths that were different from yours?

Socrates, the great philosopher from ancient Greece said, "The unexamined life is not worth living" and spent his entire life in pursuit of wisdom and understanding by asking questions and engaging others in conversations. When we start to examine our concepts of ourselves, our beliefs and how we acquired them, we see that many or most of them were taught to us; that we were like clean sheets of paper that the people and institutions mentioned wrote *their* narratives on. The net effect of these people and institutions on us is that we come into adulthood having a positive or negative concept of ourselves which in turn affect our self-esteem and self-confidence.

> **Reflection**
>
> Reflect on the people and institutions that have shaped your self-esteem.
>
> What are the positive things they have said and done that have built your self-esteem?
>
> What are the negative things they have said and done that have diminished your self-esteem?
>
> How would you defend yourself against the negative comments of these people and institutions?

How we function in the world as adults depends very much on whether we have high or low self esteem and so it is very important that we develop a self reflective process that enables us to unearth and question what we have been taught about ourselves, and ultimately to shape and redefine who we are in a way that serves our positive growth and development as human beings. Take some time and answer the Reflection questions.

Signs of High Self-Esteem

If you want to build high self esteem you need to know what it looks like in people with high self esteem. People with high self-esteem show the following traits and behaviours:

- Confident.
- Assertive. To be assertive means to respect one's rights and the rights of others.
- Accept themselves and expect others to accept them for who they are.
- Able to defend themselves against the negative comments of others. People with positive self-esteem are open to feedback from others. They do not allow others however to get away with malicious or unfair comments; nor do they allow what others say to influence how they feel about themselves.
- Comfortable with people they view as superior in some way. This comfort allows them to be generous in their opinions of their superiors and open them to emulate or be mentored by these people.
- Take full responsibility for how they feel about themselves. People with high self-esteem see themselves as powerful and capable of creating their own lives. They are actors, writers and directors in the drama of their own lives regardless of the family or context that they were born and grew up in.

Signs of Low Self-Esteem

People with low self-esteem show the following traits and behaviours:
- Anxious.

- Aggressive. Aggressive people are more concerned with their rights at the expense of the rights of others. People with low self-esteem often end up as bullies.
- Critical of themselves and others.
- People with low self-esteem have poor self talk. Oftentimes their poor self talk are the replays of the negative things they have heard about themselves from their parents, teachers, friends, and significant institutions such as media in their lives.
- Unable to cope with the negative comments of others. People with low self-esteem allow others to define them.
- Envious of others they regard as superior in some way.
- Blame others for their feelings and circumstances. Blaming others for their feelings and circumstances robs them of the power to determine their thoughts, feelings and ultimately their destiny.

Reflection

It is often said that bullies have low self esteem. Why do you think people with low self-esteem want to bully and dominate others?

How would you defend yourself against a bully?

Self Talk

Earlier we said that people with low self-esteem have poor self talk, and that oftentimes their poor self talk are the replays of the negative things they have heard about themselves from their parents, teachers, friends, and significant institutions such as media.

What we say to ourselves and how we say it will have a significant impact on the way we feel about ourselves. Jack Canfield, one of the gurus on self-esteem, poses the following question, "If I spoke to my best friend the way I talk to myself, would my best friend remain my best friend?" This question really forced me to pay attention to my self-talk and I became aware of how I berated myself in the same way that my parents berated me. The words and tone they used were the words and tone I used. So what is your answer to Jack Canfield's question?

Reflection
- Reflect on your self-talk. What do you say to yourself?
- What is more dominant for you? Positive self-talk or negative self-talk?
- What are the positive things you say to yourself?
- What are the negative things you say to yourself?
- Reflect on your inner voice. What does it sound like? Does it remind you of anyone?
- How does it make you feel about yourself?

This exercise should confirm that what you say to yourself will influence the way you feel about yourself. Positive self-talk will help you feel better about yourself.

Larry Johanson

I am the Greatest!

One of my heroes is Muhammad Ali who was brash and bold enough to declare unapologetically over and over again that "I am the Greatest!" at a time when blacks in the United States were struggling for their civil rights. For a black man to make such a declaration in that context was unheard of. At best it would subject him to scorn, ridicule and contempt and at worst it would set the establishment against him.

Nevertheless Muhammad Ali kept affirming that he was the greatest backing it up with dazzling displays of boxing prowess. In time he came to be regarded as one of the greatest boxers of all time and more importantly, as a hero around the world for his courage and example of standing up for human rights and justice. To be successful, it is said that one should model successful people and so I invite you to pause and do the following bragging exercise inspired by Muhammad Ali.

How to Brag

The aim of this exercise is to get you comfortable bragging about yourself. If you've never seen or heard Muhammad Ali brag then go to You Tube or Google "Muhammad Ali Greatest speech." This exercise requires that you step into the "energy field" of Muhammad Ali and become him in intonation and attitude.

- After you think you can imitate Muhammad Ali close your eyes, take a few deep breaths, exhale and relax.
- Think of something about yourself that you really like and admire. Get really high on yourself!
- Write about yourself in glowing and admirable terms. Compose it as a rap or poem.
- Stand in front of a full length mirror and as energetically and emphatically as possible recite your poem about yourself. How did that feel?

- If you can summon the courage to recite it in front of a live audience—family or friends, that would be even better.
- If you were unable to do the exercise, what is holding you back?

Positive Affirmations

Another way to improve self-talk and self-esteem is to create positive affirmations. Positive affirmations are positive personal statements made about one's self in the present tense. An example of a positive affirmation is the one created by Emile Coué, the famous French psychotherapist, "Everyday in every way I get better and better." Affirmations are not necessarily true at the time you make them. They are instead expressions of what you would be if you became your ideal self. Positive affirmations reinforce positive attitudes and behaviour.

How to Create Positive Affirmations

- Close your eyes. Take a few deep breaths. Exhale and relax.
- Think of five things you like about yourself or five qualities or skills you would like to develop.
- Write them down.
- Turn the statements you have written down into affirmations.
- Share your affirmations with someone who is close to you and supportive.

Positive Visualizations

Visualization is another powerful technique you can use to feel better about yourself. Positive visualization is the use of your imagination in a positive way to paint a better picture of yourself or your situation.

Visualizations are powerful because the unconscious mind does not distinguish between an imaginary and a real event.

Elite athletes and other high achievers use this technique to complement their preparation for their events. They visualize themselves being calm and relaxed, winning their events, or performing at a very high level and soaking up the accolades of the crowd. When they actually perform in their events they are not anxious and fearful because as far as their unconscious mind is concerned, they have won this event several times over.

Emile Coué, the French psychotherapist mentioned earlier, confirmed the power of visualization when he said, "When the imagination and the willpower are in conflict, are antagonistic, it is always the imagination that wins, without any exception. When the imagination and the willpower are harmoniously pulling in the same direction, irresistible force is the result."

Demonstrating the Power of Visualization

This exercise should demonstrate the power of visualization to you. You may want to work with someone who will read out the following instructions to you. The person reading the instructions should give you enough time to clearly visualize each step before moving on. You could also record the instructions and play them back.

- Close your eyes, take a deep breath and exhale, breathing out all your tensions.
- See yourself sitting at your dining table.
- On the table is a basket of fresh lemons.
- See the colors…smell them.
- Get a knife, take one of the lemons out of the basket and cut it.
- Take one half of the lemon and squeeze the juice on your tongue.

- Let the juice run back into your throat.
- Now come back into the room.

What happened as you visualized squeezing the lemon juice onto your tongue? The response of people who do this visualization exercise is that they find themselves making saliva as they imagine the tartness of the lemon juice running into the back of their throats.

The next time you know that you will be required to perform at a level where the stakes are high at a personal and professional level do what elite athletes do. Use your imagination to visualize yourself performing well. Make it as vivid as possible by engaging all your senses. What do you see, hear, and feel? Are you calm, relaxed, in control? Can you see yourself as the greatest in this situation? Run the scene over and over in your mind until you can confidently say yes to all the questions I asked and you are eager and enthusiastic to go out and "knock their socks off!" as the saying goes.

The Essence of High Self Esteem

The essence of high self-esteem according to Jack Canfield is knowing that you are capable and lovable. To be capable is to have the ability, competence, resources and skills to be successful in whatever you set out to do. To be lovable is to be attractive and worthy of love. How do you know whether you're capable and lovable? Here is an exercise that will help you determine how capable and lovable you are.

The Capable and Lovable Exercise[5]

- Get a piece of paper and divide it into two columns.

---

[5] Adapted from Jack Canfield's *How to Build High Self-Esteem*

- Label one column "Capable" and the other "Lovable."
- In the "Capable" column list the things you do well.
- In the "Lovable" column list the qualities that make you a lovable person.
- Try to fill both columns with as many abilities and skills that confirm that you are a capable and lovable person.
- Aim for at least 20 skills and qualities respectively.
- Give yourself a treat if you were able to do so.
- If you were not able to do so ask friends, family, colleagues for their feedback.
- Keep adding to the columns.

You ought to begin feeling better about yourself as you begin to see yourself as capable and lovable.

Your Achievement Log

Another activity you can do to build your self-confidence and self-esteem is to keep an Achievement Log. Your Achievement Log is a diary of your triumphs. It is a running score of all the things you have tried and succeeded at. It becomes a bank of stored successes and warm and fuzzy feelings that you can draw upon when you want to remind yourself that you are an achiever or when you want to shore up your self-confidence.

Creating your Achievement Log

- Purchase a notebook and label it "My Achievement Log."
- List the things you've achieved that you're proud of.
- Write the date when you had your achievement, the reaction of others and how you felt.
- If you cannot remember the date it is o.k. Just add the achievements to your log.

- Keep adding to your Achievement Log until you've built up a rich bank of achievements that you can draw on when you need to.

The Relationship of Self-Esteem and Self-Confidence

Self-esteem and self-confidence are very closely related and mentioned in the same breath. Self-confidence comes from a sense of competence and capability. Competence and capability are built from doing, gaining experience and expertise. To gain experience and expertise you have to take risks. Many people hold themselves back because of their fear of failure. However, the people I've known who have succeeded spectacularly also have failed more than others.

Years ago, a seminar leader colleague of mine declared triumphantly that he was failing his way to success and the statement initially baffled me until I grasped the truth of the paradox of failure. Failure is not failure if the attitude you bring to it is that it is not a judgment of you or your abilities but rather important feedback. There is the popular story of Thomas Edison, the inventor of the light bulb, who apparently conducted thousands of trials before he got it right. He never considered any of the experiments he conducted failures. They were results. He is reported to have said in relation to his efforts to invent the light bulb that "If I find 10,000 ways something won't work, I haven't failed. I am not discouraged, because every wrong attempt discarded is another step forward."

Michael Jordan, said to be one of the greatest basketball players of all time, said of his failures, "I've missed more than 9,000 shots in my career...I've lost almost 300 games...26 times I've been trusted to take the game winning shot and missed...I've failed over and over and over again in my life...And that is why I succeed."

Edison and Jordan eloquently sum up the dragon's mindset. Failure is not and will never be an option for someone with this mindset.

My Two Most Powerful Transformational Tools

The strategies that I've shared with you are very effective for developing high self esteem and self-confidence but the two most powerful tools that I've used to transform my life are zazen and loving-kindness meditation. I had the great good fortune in my youth to meet Zen master Roshi Philip Kapleau, author of *The Three Pillars of Zen*, who so struck me with his presence and serenity that I determined there and then that I wanted to be like him. I later became his student and have practiced Zen since then, for over thirty years.

Zazen is a method of focused attention and awareness that uses the breath to integrate body and mind and empty one's self[6] of everything—ideas, concepts, thoughts, emotions, perceptions—that reinforce the notion that we are separate, isolated individuals, cut off from the world around us, and in constant competition and conflict to maintain this self or identity which is based on ego. (In Strategy #5 I'll share with you how I use the breath awareness techniques in zazen to manage stress).

In the process of emptying myself of this excess baggage of ideas, thoughts, emotions, perceptions, and limiting beliefs of my conditioned mind I realized that my real self-worth is not dependent on my accomplishments, wealth, social status, ethnic origin, gender, and the many other ways in which society tries to label, measure and categorize me. I realized that my real self-worth as a human being is absolute and that this is true of everyone. It took me a long time to accept this truth and only after many years of continuously emptying myself

---

[6] To empty one's self means to release or let go of everything that binds.

of the labels and ways in which I learned to measure myself and my worth as an individual.

A great big overweening ego is just as fragile and vulnerable as an ego that is grounded in a sense of inferiority. In an ultimate sense, the ego, whether it is large or small, is the problem. Getting rid of it, or more accurately seeing into it and understanding that who we think we are is just a concept; that in fact we are a boundless field of possibilities, frees us from the suffering that accompanies our distorted perception of ourselves.

Talk show host, Oprah Winfrey, in her final show closing out 25 years of transforming people's lives, noted that the common thread that was at the root of all the issues guests on her show struggled with, whether it was addiction, anxiety, or not stepping into their greatness was a sense of being unworthy.

She emphatically told her audience that they were enough; that the fact that they were born and are living on this earth here, now, is testament to their worthiness and all they had to do was to listen for the life that they were called to live. This is the message that all the great sages and philosophers have been delivering from time immemorial—that the capacity for greatness lies within all of us and to be truly worthy is simply to acknowledge this capacity and allow it to guide us.

After struggling for six painful years to come to Enlightenment, the Buddha upon eventually coming to Enlightenment, declared, "Wonder of wonders! Intrinsically all living beings are Buddhas, endowed with Wisdom and Virtue." When we know this to be an existential fact then we will never question our worthiness, nor have any need to develop self confidence or self esteem. We will accept ourselves just the way we are, knowing that we are whole and complete

Larry Johanson

Practicing Loving-Kindness[7]

Practicing loving-kindness meditation is the other transformational tool I've used with great success. Legend has it that the Buddha introduced the practice of loving-kindness meditation to monks who came to him complaining that they were being haunted by nature spirits in the forest where they were meditating and requested that he change their location. Rather than giving them permission to change their location the Buddha taught them to direct loving-kindness to the spirits that haunted the forest. In time, this practice ended the disturbance of the spirits, who, instead of haunting the monks became their servants and allies.

Loving-kindness is also a powerful practice for transforming anger and resentment into love and acceptance. One of the issues that convinced me that I needed to transform my life was the deep anger and resentment I harboured against my parents, the situation I was born in, and what I perceived to be the unfairness of life. I realized that anger and resentment are the most corrosive emotions one can have; that they are internal enemies that rob one of one's joy and peace, not to mention one's competitive edge. The Buddha said that one who harbours hatred is like someone who drank poison wishing that it would kill his enemy.

The practice of loving-kindness comes out of the realization that we are fundamentally whole and complete and that we are inextricably connected and bound to each other in a vast matrix of interdependence. Loving-kindness is thus an all encompassing, unconditional openness and acceptance of one's self and others, and not a love based on the self serving notion of "what's in it for me" or "you scratch my back and I'll scratch yours." The irony is that most of us

---

[7] For a comprehensive discussion of the power of Loving-Kindness see Sharon Salzberg's book of the same name.

as human beings, in spite of the fact that we are driven by ego, whether that ego is expressed in being superior or inferior, are insecure and don't genuinely love and appreciate ourselves.

Loving-kindness begins with a deep appreciation of one's self and one's basic goodness as a human being. Loving-kindness replaces mindless, negative self-talk with conscious, positive affirmations directed toward ourselves and then to others. Affirmations, as we noted earlier, are strong, positive statements about one's self in the present tense. Affirmations help to reinforce positive attitudes and behaviours. Examples of affirmations are, "I am a great stress manager; I have all the tools I need to live a good life; I am free of anger and hatred; I am filled with compassion and joy; I like and appreciate myself."

To begin practicing loving-kindness, stabilize and ground yourself by focusing on your breath and as you breathe in count "one" and as you breathe out count "two". Continue in this manner all the way up to ten. When you feel calm and relaxed repeat the above affirmations, or ones you create, silently to yourself, absorbing yourself in the goodwill and generous feelings that arise out of these affirmations. Direct these feelings to yourself, saying, "May I be well, may I be happy, may I be free from stress and anxiety, may I be free from anger and hatred, may I be full of generosity and goodwill towards others."

Most of us find it difficult to direct loving and generous feelings to ourselves. The Buddha made it clear that of all the people in the entire universe who is worthy of your love, none is more worthy than you. You cannot give what you don't have, and if you don't love yourself and take care of yourself, then you won't be able to love others. Some people mistake the advice to love one's self as being narcissistic or selfish and self-involved. To love yourself is to esteem or hold yourself in high regard. Holding yourself in high regard does not mean that you put others down. All it means is that you wish the best for yourself, and in wishing the best for yourself, you wish it also for others.

I've found from experience that the more I practice loving-kindness, the clearer it is to me that to take care of myself is to take care of everyone and everything; and to take care of everyone and everything is to take care of myself. This sense of connection gives rise to empathy and compassion for one's self and others, and a more open, relaxed and generous attitude to everyone. The ultimate payoff is healing and peace for one's self.

Next, extend the goodwill and generous feelings that come out of your affirmations to your loved ones. While visualizing the person or holding them in your heart, affirm, "May he/she be happy, may he/she be well, may he/she be free from stress and anxiety, may he/she be free from danger, may he/she be full of generosity and goodwill towards others, may he/she experience the goodwill and generosity of others."

You can then extend the same wishes to strangers you come in contact with—the shopkeeper, the person sitting beside you on the bus or train. Then extend the same feelings to people you have difficulties with. The people we have difficulty with can be a real source of stress and anxiety for us and it can be quite a challenge to have generous and loving feelings for people whom we have labelled 'difficult'.

Oftentimes the people we have difficulty with also have difficulty with us, and more often than not, the qualities we don't like in a person are projections of qualities we ourselves possess. It is very important to look at ourselves and take the beam out of our eyes first before taking the mote out of the eyes of our fellow human beings.

When we have worked through sending thoughts of loving kindness and goodwill to ourselves, to our loved ones, to people we don't necessarily know but come in contact with in our daily lives—often referred to as the neutral person, and to the difficult person, we're finally ready to extend loving kindness to the whole universe. We can extend loving kindness to all people beginning with our neighbours, our region, our country, to all countries and races, all creatures who occupy the earth with us, the earth itself as a living entity and outward and beyond to the universe.

In so doing, we open and expand the capacity of our heart-mind to love and in the context of such a vast perspective, the things that irritate us and rob us of our peace, begin to seem rather small.

Summary

The Dragon's Mindset is that whole complex of right attitudes, beliefs, and habitual patterns of thinking that contribute to high self-esteem and self-confidence. It cuts through all the mental and emotional obstacles that stand in your way. The following strategies will help you build the Dragon's Mindset that is impervious to failure:

- Engage in positive self-talk.
- Use positive visualization.
- Develop an inventory of things you do well.
- List the qualities that make you a lovable person.
- Maintain an Achievement Log.
- Fail your way to success.
- Do zazen or any other form of contemplative prayer or meditation that helps you to empty your mind of the way you label and categorize yourself.
- Practice loving-kindness meditation for yourself and others.

In Strategy #3 you'll learn how to Find Your Mission and Purpose in life.

STRATEGY #3. FIND YOUR MISSION AND PURPOSE

"If you don't know where you're going any road will take you there."
Cheshire Cat—Alice in Wonderland

The above quote was Cheshire Cat's response to Alice who came upon a fork in the road and asked him for directions. Cheshire Cat's response was that his directions depended on where Alice wanted to go. Alice replied that she didn't know where she wanted to go, hence Cheshire Cat's response.

Like Alice, many of us drift aimlessly through life without any sense of where we want to go, what we want to do or become, and why. I've done seminars all over the world and have met many people who are unhappy with their jobs or their positions in life. Oftentimes, they are bitter and angry and see themselves as victims of circumstance. The root of their unhappiness lies in the fact that they are not clear about their mission and purpose in life. They've settled for living in default mode, going along to get along instead of charting their own path and forging their own destiny.

Whenever I was confronted with unhappy people in a seminar I would ask, "How many of you have a written mission statement that you consult on a regular basis?" Invariably only about 5-10 out of every 100, or about 5% to 10% of individuals in the room, said they had a mission statement. Ironically, all of them said "yes" when I probed further whether their companies or departments have mission statements.

They also knew the purpose and importance of mission statements for their companies or departments, yet they never saw the importance of one in helping them determine the direction of their lives.

Of the 5%-10% who said they had a mission statement, fewer still had it as a written document that they consulted on an ongoing basis as they chart their path through life. I've also found that the individuals who said they had a written mission statement were invariably the ones who were more in control of their lives. They seemed more enthusiastic and optimistic about their lives and future. They were in careers they chose; were more widely traveled; and had more disposable income. This seems to be the case regardless of the country, culture, and occupation of the respondents. It is clear therefore that if you want to achieve your dreams you need to determine your mission and purpose in life and write your personal mission statement.

To gain clarity about your mission and purpose in life you have to confront and answer what I call the **BIG QUESTIONS**. These are:

- Who am I?
- What am I doing here?
- How am I going to live my life or spend my time while I am here?
- What do I want to be remembered for, or what legacy do I want to leave behind?

These questions are not easy to answer. They take a lot of digging and soul searching and while they may occur to most of us, many of us don't spend the time to find the answers. It is often said that we spend more time planning our vacations than planning our life. It is eminently worthwhile answering these questions however, because once you are clear about the answers, you are in a position to write your personal mission statement. And having a written mission statement helps you to clarify your purpose. So before going any further, pause and reflect on these questions. They may also be a source of rich dialogue between you and your spouse, your children, and your friends.

What is a Personal Mission Statement?

A personal mission statement is your personal blueprint of your purpose in life. It outlines your goals and your roles; what you want to be, what you want to do, and the values and principles which will guide you in how you go about achieving your mission and purpose.

The Purpose of a Personal Mission Statement.

Why should we bother writing our personal mission statement? A personal mission statement:

- Defines our purpose.
- Puts our dreams in focus.
- Gives us direction in life.
- Gives us stability and control over our lives.
- Becomes a standard against which we measure our success.

How to find your own Mission and Purpose.

Here are some process steps that will help you to find your own mission. Each step will help you sharpen your self awareness, a necessary factor in finding your mission.

- Know yourself.
- Clarify your values.
- Clarify your beliefs.
- Discover your gifts.
- Visualize the life you want to live.
- Map a strategy to fulfill your mission.

Know Yourself

Close your eyes and become centered in yourself. You are going to take a good inventory of yourself. Here are some questions to guide you.

- Am I generally happy or sad? Why?
- Am I a shy or friendly person? Why?
- What kind of people do I like to hang out with? Why?
- What were the happiest times of my life? Why?
- What were the saddest times of my life? Why?
- What are my talents?
- What are the things I love to do and do well?
- What are my strong religious beliefs?
- What are my strong beliefs about how society should function—justice, equality, service?
- How do I feel about money?
- How much of my attitude towards money comes from my parents?

Clarifying your Values

To clarify your values is to become clear and specific about them. Your values are the moral principles and standards which govern your life—e.g. Honesty, kindness, fairness.

> **Reflection on your Values**
>
> - Imagine that you have more money than you could possibly spend.
> - What would you do with your life?
> - How would you spend your money?
> - What values can you recognize?

Clarifying your Beliefs

To clarify your beliefs is also to become clear about them. Your beliefs are the ideas, assumptions and opinions you accept as true.

> **Reflection on your Beliefs**
>
> - Imagine you met an alien from another planet who asked you to share your most cherished beliefs. What are those beliefs?
> - If it challenged you on those beliefs, which would be the most difficult ones to give up?
> - Which would be the easiest to give up?

Larry Johanson

How to Discover Your Gifts

It is very important that your Mission Statement reflects your gifts and talents. Your gifts and talents give you an indication of what you are born to do. It is therefore very important to know what they are. So how do you know that you are blessed with a particular gift? What is a gift anyway? A gift is a talent or ability that you are born with which enable you to do certain mental or physical activities effortlessly which others struggle with. A gift could also be referred to as a type of "smarts" or intelligence.

The answers to the following questions will give you clues to what your gifts are.

- What are the subjects, things in which you have a deep interest?
- What are the things you like doing, and which come naturally to you?
- What are the gifts that people who know you well say you possess?
- What would your choice be if you were to choose between working with people and working with things? Give reasons.

Earlier we said that gifts could be referred to as a type of "smarts" or intelligence. Researchers have found that there are many different forms of intelligence or "smarts" which are not measured by traditional IQ tests and that all of us are strong in at least one of these "smarts." This means that we all have the potential to be good, even great at something, provided you work at developing this gift or "smarts." So what are these "smarts?"

The Seven Types of Smarts[8]

The following are regarded as the seven types of "smarts."

1. Music smarts.
2. Body smarts.
3. People smarts.
4. Self-smarts.
5. Picture smarts.
6. Word smarts.
7. Logic smarts.

Reflection

As you read about the "smarts" think of the people you know who have this "smarts". How do they use it?

Where would you rate yourself on a scale of 1-10 where "1" is "poor" and "10" is "excellent?" Has anyone ever complimented you for having this "smarts"?

---

[8] This notion of the Seven Types of Smarts is based on the work of Dr. Howard Gardner, the Harvard researcher who developed the concept of multiple intelligences and identified the seven distinct ways we learn and know about reality.

Music Smarts

- People with Music Smarts have the ability to sing and use musical instruments.
- Can recognize and use rhythmic and tonal patterns.
- Become singers, composers, players in orchestras and bands and music teachers.

Body Smarts

- People with Body Smarts have the ability to execute activities that require excellent bodily control and coordination.
- People with Body Smarts become athletes, actors, professional dancers and mimes.

People Smarts

- Individuals with People Smarts are good verbal and non-verbal communicators. They work well with others on teams or in groups.
- They can pick up on people's moods, temperaments and motivations and empathize with their feelings, fears, and beliefs.
- People Smarts is highly developed in counselors, teachers, therapists, religious leaders and politicians.

Self Smarts

- People with Self Smarts are in touch with their moods, feelings and emotions.
- They can step back and observe themselves interacting with others and are aware of their impact.
- They can sense a connection to a reality that is larger than them and are aware of the wholeness of nature.
- Self Smarts is highly developed in philosophers, psychiatrists, spiritual counselors and gurus.

Picture Smarts

- People with Picture Smarts can see things in 3 dimensions.
- They have abilities to paint, draw, sculpt, navigate, make maps, and create architectural plans.
- Picture Smarts is highly developed in architects, graphic designers, map makers, industrial designers, painters and sculptors.

Word Smarts

- People with Word Smarts are comfortable with language in its various forms.
- This includes storytelling, poetry, reading and writing, humor, symbolic thinking, grammar, metaphors, similes and abstract reasoning.
- Poets, playwrights, storytellers, novelists, public speakers and comedians have highly developed Word Smarts.

Logic Smarts

- People with Logic Smarts are great at math. They are comfortable with "scientific thinking" which draws logical conclusions or makes generalizations from sets of information.
- They can recognize patterns, work with numbers, and geometric shapes, and see relationships between separate and distinct pieces of information.
- Scientists, computer programmers, accountants, lawyers, bankers, and mathematicians all have Logic Smarts.

EQ—Another Type of Smarts

Word Smarts and Logic Smarts are the only two types of intelligence that have been measured and valued as an indication of one's IQ. The emphasis in western education systems is on developing these two types of intelligence.

EQ or Emotional Intelligence is another type of smarts which is now regarded as perhaps even more important than IQ in predicting the probability of one becoming an achiever. EQ is a combination of Self Smarts and People Smarts. It is said that whereas IQ gets you in the door of a company, what distinguishes those who eventually make it to the executive suite is their possession of EQ.

EQ can be defined as "one's awareness of one's emotional states, the ability to effectively manage these states and to help others do the same for themselves." EQ is regarded as one of the most important intelligences because it determines your happiness. It makes sense that if you are self aware and know how to get along with others you are likely to be happier.

Create Your Vision Board

In Strategy #2 we spoke about the power of visualization and one of the process steps outlined in discovering your mission was visualizing the life you want to live. One of the ways to implement this step is to create a Vision Board.

A Vision Board takes your mission statement or dreams from the unseen realm of the imagination to the physical realm of sight. Seeing what you want reminds you of your mission and purpose and fires you up to achieve them.

To create a Vision Board you will need the following:

- A sheet of Bristol board.
- A glue stick.
- A pair of scissors.
- Old newspapers, magazines and pictures.

Cut out and assemble pictures based on the following consideration:

- Imagine yourself living the life you ideally want to live 5, 10, 15 years from now?
- What job are you doing?
- What kind of house are you living in?
- What kind of car are you driving?
- What gifts and abilities are you using?
- Who benefits from those gifts and abilities?
- What would you want people to say about you?
- After you have assembled your Vision Board, put it in a prominent place where you can see it every day and let it inspire you to pursue your dreams.

Your Mission and Your Career

A formula for achieving your dreams is to choose a career that expresses or allows you to live your mission. Your career is a unique expression of who you are in the world. It is the activity that allows you to use your gifts and talents to serve humanity and yourself while expressing your values.

Happy and fulfilled people do what they love and love what they do. Their careers become vehicles to fulfill their missions. The fact that they get paid for what they love to do is a huge bonus.

A Career vs. a Job

It is important to draw a distinction between a career and a job. The choice of a career is one of the most important decisions that you can make in your life. The choice is as important as the person you decide to marry, according to the famous psychoanalyst, Sigmund Freud.

Your financial well-being and fulfillment depends on how rewarding your career is.

To choose a career, you need to consider your personality traits, interests, values and talents. You will require in many instances, long and expensive training and education.

A job, on the other hand, does not require much training or education. It can be done by almost anyone, and does not provide much room for personal growth and development. Over the years, the word "job" has morphed into the acronym "J.O.B." which stands for, "Just Over Broke." It is a bitter recognition of those who are caught on the treadmill of low paying, unsatisfying work that barely covers their basic needs and none of their need for Self-Actualization.

Maslow's Hierarchy of Needs

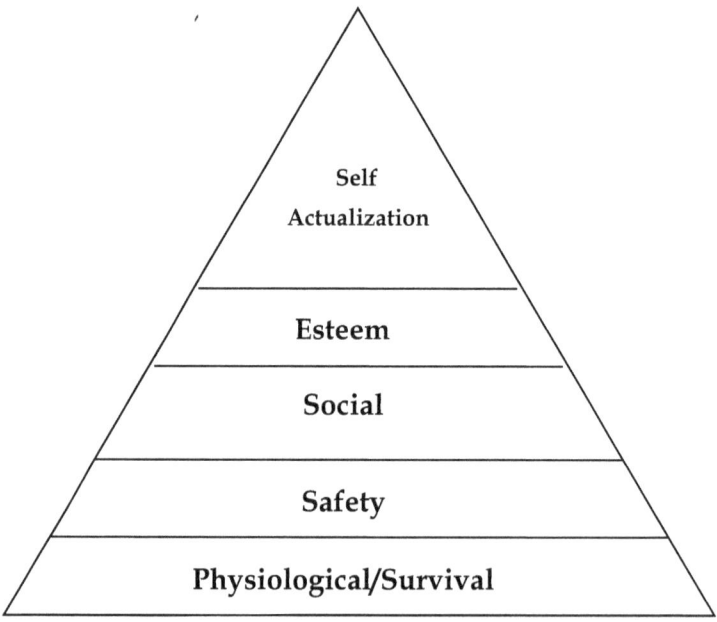

As you consider the choice of a career, it is perhaps useful to consider Abraham Maslow's Hierarchy of Needs.

Abraham Maslow was a psychologist who pioneered studies on personality and motivation. Maslow argued that needs are primary influences on the individual's motivations, priorities and behaviours. Needs create tension and the goal of behaviour is to reduce the discomfort caused by unsatisfied needs. Unsatisfied needs are therefore primary motivators and are fulfilled in ascending order from the most basic to the most advanced.

At the bottom of the hierarchy, (see diagram) are physiological/survival needs. Examples of such needs are food, shelter and clothing. Then comes safety needs. Everyone has a basic need to be safe. We need to be protected from emotional and physical harm. We need safe schools, safe neighborhoods, clean water, and regular medical check-ups. People in developed countries such as Canada, satisfy these needs relatively easily and assume that other people in the world have the same privileges. This is not so.

Still further up the hierarchy are social needs. Social needs are interpersonal needs; the need for relationships; the need to be accepted; the need to be liked and to belong to groups. After the social needs are met, we look to satisfy the esteem needs. Esteem needs are the needs to be seen as worthy; to excel; to gain recognition and rewards.

At the very top of Maslow's hierarchy are Self-Actualizing needs. These are the most challenging needs to satisfy. They involve creative expression; personal growth; striving for one's personal best; striving for autonomy and freedom; making choices and taking responsibility for those choices. At this level people do what they love and love what they do.

The idea is to choose a career that satisfies all of these needs. People in low paying, unsatisfying jobs are trapped at the bottom of the hierarchy and work mostly to satisfy their basic needs. If you follow the strategies outlined in this book you will have the best chance of satisfying all your needs, including your Self-Actualization needs.

Writing Your Personal Mission Statement

You now have all the tools to write a mission statement that reflects your values and beliefs and takes into consideration your gifts and talents. You also now know why it is important to write a mission statement. Review the answers to the questions you were asked and write your personal mission statement.

Writing your Personal Mission Statement is a major step on the road to realizing your dreams. Your Personal Mission Statement will help you to set the goals and activities you need to reach for and complete if you are to live your best life. After you have written your Personal Mission Statement share it with people you are close to and put it in a prominent place along with your Vision Board. Consult it on a regular basis, especially when you need to determine the best use of your time, which we will be exploring next in Strategy #4.

A Mission Statement for Everyone

I was taking my son Matthew, who may have been seven or eight years old at the time, to a soccer practice when out of the blue he asked, "Dad what must I do when I grow up?" He seemed to have given the question deep thought and so instead of rattling off a quick response such as "Lawyer" or "Doctor", which most parents want their kids to be, I paused for a moment to consider what I really wanted for him. Immediately I thought that what I really wanted for him was for him to be healthy, wealthy, wise and happy regardless of what he did in life and that was my response.

For the rest of the trip I broke down for him what I meant by saying that I wanted him to be healthy, wealthy, wise and happy. I think it is safe to say that this is what we all want for ourselves. These are all core goals that can be incorporated into our mission statement. Of course, to be healthy, wealthy, wise and happy probably means different things to different people and I broke it down for him as follows.

Health is a basic and fundamental resource and includes physical, mental, emotional and spiritual health. Physical health requires proper nutrition, exercise, sleep. Mental health involves clear thinking, grounded in reality and logic. Emotional health is about having self-worth and self-esteem, being comfortable in one's skin and having a sense of loving connection to the world and others. Spiritual health is having a connection to a Higher Power however you define It.

To be wealthy is to have a certain measure of financial security, enough to exercise a certain amount of freedom and choice in one's life; "to be able to pay the bills and have some thrills", according to Joel Bauer, one of my mentors. To be wealthy means also to be rich in love and to have deep and meaningful relationships. Above all, to have the ability and the means to create the life you want for yourself and loved ones at any time and in whatever circumstance you find yourself. It is often said that the richest people in the world would be able to recover their wealth if they lost it all because of the intangible resources they possess.

Wisdom, I explained, is the capacity to integrate and apply the knowledge gathered from all the available sources—rational, intuitive, emotional and practical—in elegant ways that emphasize one's fundamental humanity and encompasses living with love, joy, compassion and equanimity.

Happiness is a deep, open affirmation of "Yes!" to life and its myriad experiences. I always made the assumption that being healthy, wealthy and wise was enough but many philosophers and deep thinkers whom I regarded as wise weren't necessarily happy. Some of them became mired in deep despair and would have been considered as a little crazy.

Reflection

- Take some time to drill down deeper and explore what it means to you to be healthy, wealthy, wise and happy.
- What are the steps you would take to achieve these goals?

Summary

Finding your mission and purpose is one of the critical steps to living a happy and fulfilled life. The process involves the following steps:

- Digging deep within to find answers to the big questions only you can answer for yourself.
- Identifying your gifts and talents and figuring out how best to use your gifts and talents to serve and enrich others.
- Serving and enriching others will serve and enrich you also.

In Strategy #4 you'll learn how to Manage and Invest Your Time Wisely.

STRATEGY #4. MANAGE AND INVEST YOUR TIME WISELY

Great is the matter of birth and death
Life slips quickly by
Time waits for no one
Wake up! Wake up!
Don't waste a moment

(Inscription on the wooden block at the entrance of the meditation hall at the Toronto Zen Centre).

My father had spent the day in bed listening to the horse races on the radio. He was an avid gambler and the only reason he was home this Saturday was because he was recovering from an accident and couldn't go to the bar and the off track betting station to drink with his buddies and gamble on the horses. After the races were over he suddenly began to cough up blood and we rushed him to the hospital.

Prior to his departure he took off a watch which he prized deeply and looking me deeply in the eyes handed it to me as if to say he wouldn't need it anymore. I had a distinct feeling that he was saying goodbye to me and the offer of the watch was a gesture of reconciliation and asking for forgiveness. A deep chasm existed between us because of his verbal and physical abuse and at the time I didn't care for reconciling with him. He died that weekend. I gave the watch to my half-brother who promptly went out and pawned it.

I later recounted this story to my sister Myrna whom I loved and adored. She was sad that I had given up the watch and held on to the resentments I had for my father. When she died she left her watch, a man's watch, for me. Knowing her, I knew the symbolism of her leaving the watch. She wanted to remind me that life was short and time fast and fleeting. It is therefore important that we get on with living our lives as fully as possible and cleaning up our relationships with our loved ones, no matter how difficult it is for us, as our lives are over in a flash.

In my case I've had four close calls with death, one of which was the experience I recounted earlier of having the car I was driving with my son totalled by a drunk driver. The other instances were equally dramatic where in one moment I was fine and in another my life was suddenly in danger. The time to get on with accomplishing our mission and purpose is NOW!

Omar Khayyam, the great Persian poet, wrote:

The Moving Finger writes; and, having writ,
Moves on: nor all thy Piety nor Wit
Shall lure it back to cancel half a Line,
Nor all thy Tears wash out a Word of it.

Time is like the Moving Finger. It moves forward inexorably, inevitably, and we can do nothing to turn it back by even a nano second. A sure sign of its relentless forward march is that we grow up and grow old. Our youthful energy and exuberance wanes like the moon and we eventually pass on.

Time is, in every sense, a non-renewable resource. Those who spend it wisely and invest in activities that will help them realize their dreams, benefit handsomely. Those who squander it in idle pursuits soon find themselves trapped in a swamp of under-achievement, lost opportunity and unrealized potential.

To be successful, it is necessary to discipline one's self in mastering and managing one's time. To manage and invest your time wisely you will learn the following:

- How to set SMART goals and the characteristics of SMART goals
- Determine priorities using the 80/20 Rule (a.k.a. the Pareto Principle)
- Create a Priority Matrix by defining what is "Important" and "Urgent" and apply the Matrix to setting goals and priorities.
- How to overcome procrastination; delay gratification; and complete unpleasant tasks.

Time – The Stuff of Life

Benjamin Franklin, the great American statesman whom we met earlier, said, "Dost thou love Life? Then do not squander Time. For Time is the stuff Life is made of." This is indeed a profound observation. As I understand it, Franklin is saying here that time is life; life is time. They cannot be separated from each other. When we run out of time, we run out of life. When my father took off his watch and handed it to me he was saying that his time was up and so he wouldn't need a watch to measure it anymore.

How Achievers Use Time

Achievers realize that time equals life and that it is more valuable than money. They understand that every day Life deposits twenty four hours in their time bank and they can either choose to invest it wisely, or spend it foolishly.

The difference between achievers and underachievers is that achievers *invest* their time wisely in daily activities that will bring them dividends in the long run, while underachievers *spend* their time in trivial pursuits.

It is important that you know whether you are investing your time wisely or spending it foolishly. A good exercise is to keep a daily time use table to track how you are using your time. What are you doing from the moment you get up in the morning to the time you go to bed at nights?

Use the *Time Use Table* below to track how you spend your time. You may create one that covers all the activities in your day. How much of your time is invested in activities that will bring you dividends in the long run? What are those activities? How much of your time is spent gossiping on the phone; surfing the internet; watching television; hanging out at the mall; playing video games; sleeping?

Time Use Table

Date	Activity	Time Spent

The 80/20 Rule

The 80/20 Rule, also known as the Pareto Principle, is named after Vilfredo Pareto (1848-1823), an Italian economist, who observed in a study on land distribution in Italy, that 80% of the land was owned by 20% of the population.

Pareto found that this ratio applies to almost anything and can be summed up in the proposition that 80% of results or consequences flow from 20% of causes. Or 80% of the value in a set comes from 20% of the items. This proposition holds true when applied to every-day activities. For example, 80% of the production in a company comes from 20% of the staff. As well, 20% of your daily activities give 80% of your results.

The advantage of applying the 80/20 Rule is that it helps you determine what is vital and what is trivial and prevents you from spending your time quite literally in trivial pursuits.

The diagram on the next page gives a graphic illustration of the 80/20 Rule.

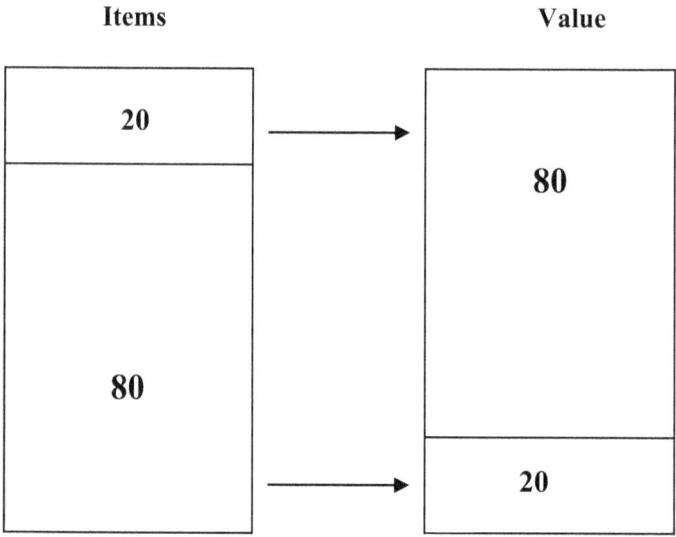

How to Determine Priority

The best way to determine the priority of a task is to weigh how important it is against how urgent it is.

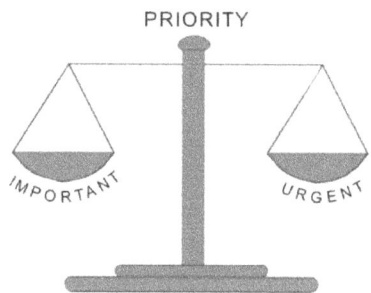

> **Reflection**
>
> - How would you apply Pareto's Principle to setting your goals and daily activities?
> - If 20% of your daily activities will give you an 80% return, what does that mean for the remaining 80% of your activities?

Important vs. Urgent Priorities

- Important priorities are your first priorities. They are the activities that help you achieve your mission and your goals.
- Urgent priorities are pressing, in-your-face priorities that demand immediate attention.

A Priority Matrix

The following is a Priority Matrix which categorizes priorities on the basis of whether they are important or urgent.

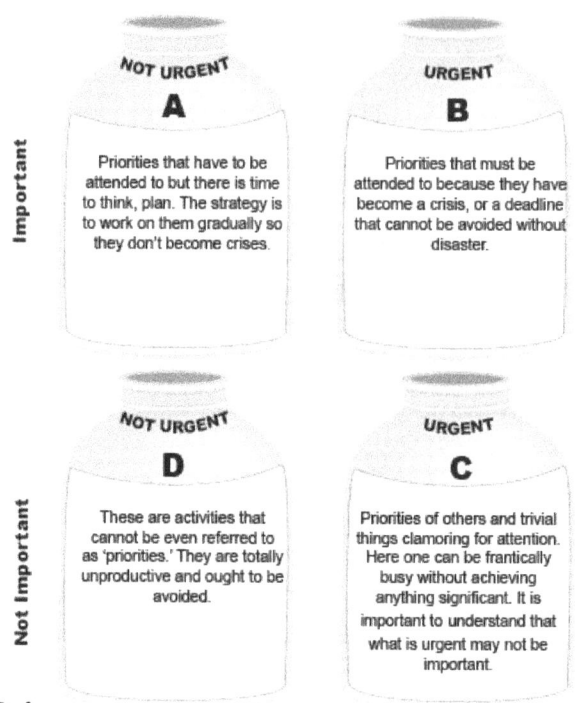

It is obvious that 'priorities' that can be classified as "Not important" and "Not Urgent" should not even merit your consideration. Be aware also of priorities which are "Not Important" and "Urgent" as these are often the priorities which others impose on you.

Priorities which are "Important" but "Not Urgent" are oftentimes the priorities which reflect your mission and which carry you towards your dreams on completing them.

Priorities which are "Important" and "Urgent" usually happen as a result of procrastination, poor planning or an unexpected occurrence. These priorities are more the exception than the rule if one is managing one's time effectively and setting goals in keeping with one's deepest mission and purpose.

Ordering Your Priorities Exercise

The following are a list of activities which fall into the various task jars of the Priority Matrix above. Place each activity in the appropriate task jar below.

- Planning, goal setting.
- Unimportant phone calls from friends.
- Car breaks down.
- Excessive TV/video games.
- Late for work.
- Relaxation.
- Turning in a project due today.
- Start working on next week's assignment.
- Gossiping.
- Building key relationships.
- Begin studying for tomorrow's exams.
- Exercise.
- Hanging out at the mall.
- Interruptions.
- Laundry.
- Friend injures self.
- Going to the movies.
- Solving other people's small problems.

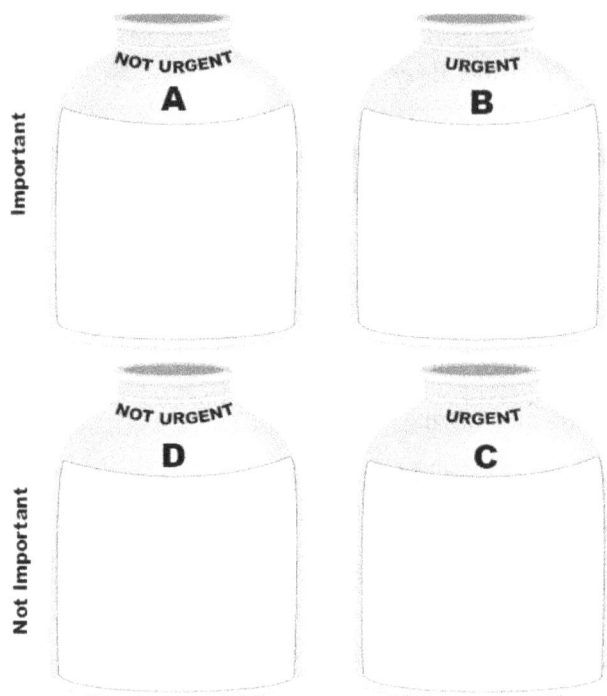

Inhabitants of the Matrix

Different individuals inhabit different areas of the matrix. Below are the types of individuals who inhabit the Matrix and their characteristics.

Creating a Weekly 'To Do' List

One of the ways to stay proactive and in control of your time and your goals is to create a weekly 'To Do' list. The advantage of doing a weekly 'to do' list is that it gives you a better perspective on your long term priorities. It allows you to put your daily tasks and activities into the larger framework of what's important in your life.

The best time to do a weekly 'to do' list is on a Friday afternoon. The last hour of a Friday afternoon is usually a winding down time for people. They are looking forward to the weekend; to relaxing and having fun with family and friends. You could use this last hour to review how the week went and create your list for the following week.

> **Action Steps**
>
> - Create a Task and Prioity Table like the one shown. Insert the number of rows that correspond to the number of tasks and activities you want to list. List the tasks and activities you would like to accomplish for the upcoming week.
>
> - Determine the priority of the activity by assigning it a letter "A"; "B"; "C" or "D" which corresponds to the matrix jar in which that activity falls.
>
> - Transfer the list you've created to the Weekly 'To Do' table in the appropriate time/day slot.

Task and Priority Table

Items	Priority	Time Estimate

Weekly 'To Do' Table

Time	Sun	Mon	Tue	Wed	Thur	Fri	Sat
5 a.m. to 9 a.m.							
9 a.m. to 12 noon							
12 noon to 5 p.m.							
5 p.m. to midnight							

Prime Time

Now that you've been introduced to the idea of scheduling the best time to do the activities that you have compiled for your weekly 'To Do' list you now need to be introduced to the concept of prime time.

Prime time is

- Your best time.
- When you're most energetic.
- When you're mentally alert.
- When you feel good.

Creating a weekly 'To Do' list and setting the date and time that you intend to accomplish your tasks and activities is part of your overall goal setting process. In setting your goals there are four questions you need to ask.

1. Will this goal help me fulfill my potential?
2. Will this goal help me achieve my mission?
3. Will this goal matter a year from now?
4. What price am I prepared to pay to achieve this goal?

> **Prime Time Action Steps**
>
> Based on how we've described prime time, what time of the day is your prime time?
>
> Review your 'To Do' list. Which activities would you classify as activities you would do in your prime time?
>
> Where would you put your prime time activities in the Priority Matrix?
>
> What would cause a prime time activity to fall into task jar 'B'?

To ensure that you set goals that fulfill these criteria, time management experts suggest an easy way to set goals whose initial letters spell out the word "SMART GOALS" and reminds us of the characteristics of "SMART GOALS." So what are the characteristics of "SMART GOALS"?

Characteristics of Smart Goals

Specific	Give direction
Measurable	Owned
Attainable	Attention
Realistic	Long/short term
Time-bound	Success

A ***specific*** goal outlines exactly what you want to accomplish. So instead of wanting to become rich, a specific goal would define exactly what "rich" means in terms of the amount of money you want.

A ***measurable*** goal sets a yard stick by which you can judge the success of your goals. In the case of someone wanting to become rich, the criteria may be to have a net worth of $1 million.

An ***attainable*** goal is one that you can achieve given the resources, abilities and motivation you possess. Attainable goals may require that you challenge yourself to reach beyond your limitations, but nevertheless, they are still attainable.

A ***realistic*** goal is similar to an attainable goal in that it is "doable", given your resources and the conditions under which you are going to attempt to achieve it. For example, to cram for an exam the night before, in the hope that you will pass, when passing would require that you master the concepts over a semester, is foolish, to say the least.

A ***time-bound*** goal has a definite deadline that you are committed to meeting. Many people, in setting goals, default to the "someday I will…" proposition. Unfortunately, "someday" never comes for them. The difference between wishful thinking and a time-bound goal is the difference between becoming an achiever and being a dreamer who cannot be taken seriously.

Smart goals *give* you *direction*. You know exactly where you want to go and what you have to do to get there.

Smart goals are *owned* by you. They are not imposed on you by anyone and you don't pursue them because they will please someone in your life.

Smart goals capture your *attention*. You are focused and concentrated in the pursuit of them. You are fired up; passionate about achieving that goal and you will do anything that is ethical, moral and legal to achieve it.

Smart goals have *long* and *short term* milestones. Long term milestones may be measured in years. Short term milestones may be measured in weeks or months.

Smart goals lead to *success* and achievement. Success and achievement are the summits that all achievers and dragons seek to scale throughout the course of their lives.

SMART GOALS Action Steps

- In Strategy #3 you were taken through the process of developing a mission statement that reflected your values and your talents and the best way to harness them in pursuit of your dreams.
- Go back to your mission statement, and based on what you wrote, list a minimum of five SMART GOALS you need to accomplish in order to achieve your mission.
- Do you have any time frame for the achievement of these goals?

- Which ones can you begin today? Which ones are dependent on you achieving a short term goal before you can achieve those?
- Which goals will give you the best return for your efforts in the short term?

Procrastination

One of the most negative and unproductive habits that can derail your ambition and thwart your drive for achievement is the habit of procrastination. To procrastinate, according to the *Collins English Dictionary* is "to put off or defer an action until a later time." We procrastinate for several reasons. These include:

- Poor time management.
- The task seems too big.
- Fear of failure.
- Lack of a compelling reason (mission, vision) to complete the task.

The Danger of Procrastination

One of my grand aunt's favourite quotes was "Procrastination is the thief of time." Only after understanding how precious time is, have I come to appreciate the grave implications the habit of procrastination has for achieving one's goals and ultimately one's mission in life. Do you procrastinate and what are the things you procrastinate on? Pause for a few moments and reflect on this. Why do you procrastinate?

In William Shakespeare's *Julius Caesar*, Brutus makes the following observation:

There is a tide in the affairs of men,
Which taken at the flood, leads on to fortune.
Omitted, all the voyage of their life is bound in shallows and misery.

Anyone who wants to achieve their dreams should inscribe these words on their hearts.

Achievers have a knack for being ready to greet the tide of opportunity when it rolls in and invariably are successful in their endeavours. Oftentimes, people look on in disbelief at how fortunate these achievers are in being in the right place at the right time. A deeper look however, shows that these people are "lucky" only because they are prepared and acted decisively when it was required of them.

Oprah Winfrey defines luck as "preparation meeting opportunity." The danger of procrastination is that you run the risk of missing the tide of opportunity, which may be the only chance you ever get to realize your dream. You're truly left in the shallows of underachievement and the miseries of unrealized potential if your tide rolls in and you haven't caught it, so…**DON'T PROCRASTINATE**.

How to Overcome Procrastination

The question is, "how do we overcome procrastination?" Here are some strategies you can use.

- Remind yourself of your Mission. Stephen Covey in the *Seven Habits of Highly Effective People* advises to "Begin with the end in mind." Your Mission is this end. Just imagine the sense of accomplishment and satisfaction when you achieve this end!
- Plan and schedule the task.
- Set a deadline.

- Break the task into bite sized pieces. It is said that the only way to consume an elephant is by one piece at a time.
- Find a partner that you can work with to motivate each other and become accountable to.
- Give yourself a reward when you accomplish a task.

A Timely and Final Thought on Time

Most human beings, whether they are achievers or under-achievers, naturally seek the easy way out and avoid work that is dull or difficult. Achievers know however, that doing what they dislike is often the way to realizing their dreams. They discipline themselves and focus on the goal, rather than the unpleasant task at hand, and are rewarded for their discipline with success.

Underachievers are not so. They yield to the temptation of not doing the dull or difficult task. They seek instead to satisfy their immediate craving for ease and pleasure and end up sabotaging themselves in the long run. There is definitely something to be said for paying your dues.

Summary

The clock begins to tick from the moment you draw your first breath and embark on the journey of your life. Time is synonymous with life and is therefore the most precious resource you possess. Invest it wisely instead of spending it freely and foolishly and you will be handsomely rewarded. "Don't waste a moment", as the inscription on the wooden block at the Toronto Zen Centre advises.

In Strategy #5 you'll learn how to Breathe Your Stress Away.

Larry Johanson

STRATEGY #5. BREATHE YOUR STRESS AWAY

"It is not stress that kills us; it is our reaction to it." Hans Selye

Your aspiration to become a dragon, to leap beyond your limitations and summit the Mount Everest of your dreams will take you out of your comfort zone. Guaranteed. Every one of the leaps I took which landed me in a different dimension was accompanied by great fear and trembling. When I decided to go to university I worried whether I had the capacity to take on the rigours of academic work and there were patches in my Masters where I thought that I couldn't do it. It wasn't just the issue of taking on a large workload but also coping with one of the coldest winters in a hundred years the first year when I came to Canada, and having very little money.

Similarly, my first assignment as a seminar leader was to do a two week gig in Australia. I had just become a father and devastated by being laid off. This was an opportunity to embark on a new career path. The stakes were high at both a personal and professional level, and in spite of my anxiety of being so far away from home, in a strange context where I was expected to perform at a very high level, I had to take the leap, trusting somehow that I would be o.k.

There were days in the midst of preparing when I would take the globe I had and trace the distance from Canada to Australia and swallow hard.

In both contexts I performed very well. I had the distinction of offering the best thesis by a foreign student in the year I graduated with my Masters and I garnered an arm load of rave reviews from people who attended my seminars in Australia. These were pivotal moments in my life which I look back on with fondness and a certain measure of pride. This was certainly a long way from Brentford Road. There were friends I knew who when faced with the possibility of escaping the narrow confines of their contexts, shrank back in fear and buried themselves literally in the moss at the bottom of their stagnant fish bowls.

So what gave me the ability to take on those challenges? Earlier I mentioned my good fortune in discovering *The Three Pillars of Zen* and subsequently meeting its author, Zen master Roshi Philip Kapleau. When I read the book I knew instantly that I was on to something and began immediately doing zazen. By the time I encountered the book and learned how to meditate, I was stretched so taut that I was barely holding myself together. The difficult years I had in my youth had begun to take their toll and I was still in my teens!

The immediate benefit of meditating was that I had deep, dreamless, refreshing sleep and the high levels of physical and emotional strain I felt gradually began to subside. Another benefit was that I could study with a great deal of concentration and whenever I found myself in stressful situations I knew how to literally breathe my stress away. This skill that I had learned became my secret weapon, the staff I leaned upon when I needed support. Over time I became more and more capable of drawing strength from within, relying less and less on others to provide emotional support.

This skill has literally saved my life. Even though alcohol and marijuana were readily available in my environment I never relied on them to help me manage stress even when my peers and members of my family became heavily dependent on them. My response to stress is to meditate, not medicate. Later on I will share some breath awareness exercises that you can use for yourself when stressed.

You can easily become a victim of your own drive for success and achievement if you do not know how to handle the pressures, stresses and strains you are bound to encounter. I've known university students who had nervous breakdowns and colleagues in the corporate context who had to go off on short and long term disability because they couldn't cope with the challenges they faced in their lives.

They failed because they simply did not have the skills and the abilities to manage stress. Knowing how to manage stress is a basic life skill and a pre-requisite for achievement. What use is it to gain success at the expense of your health? By learning how to manage stress you are able to neutralize and absorb internal and external pressures; develop the resilience to bounce back from failure and disappointment, and go on to claim the accolades and recognition that comes with your achievement.

In this strategy we'll explore the following topics:

1. Define what stress is.
2. Distinguish between good stress and bad stress.
3. Examine the role of perception in experiencing stress.
4. Help you identify your stressors.
5. Offer some relaxation techniques.
6. Strategies to manage change.

What is Stress?

Dr. Hans Selye (1907-1982), the Canadian pioneer in stress research defined stress as "a non-specific response of the organism to any pressure or demand." A non-specific response means that different people will have different responses when faced by the same situation. Some may laugh or cry; others may get angry or find deep reservoirs of calm capability.

According to Sara Zeff Geber, author of *How To Manage Stress For Success*, stress is, "a state of imbalance between demands from inside or outside sources and our perceived abilities to meet those demands."

From a layman's perspective, "stress" is a catchall word that describes a stretched to the limit, can't take it anymore feeling when one is taxed beyond one's physical, emotional, spiritual and intellectual limits.

The Difference between Good Stress and Bad Stress

In defining stress however, we need to be aware of the difference between good stress and bad stress. Experts on stress argue that stress itself is not a bad thing. It is how we deal with stress that determines whether we experience it is good or bad.

Good stress, also known as eustress, increases performance and efficiency. For example, Olympic athletes become Olympic champions because they are able to rise to the big moment and use the pressure they experience to perform well. They are able to get into a "flow" state which many describe as a focused and effortless state of peak performance.

I experienced this "flow" state once while playing soccer in my youth. I was physically fit and strong and could run very fast. I played left defensive back and because of my speed my coach used me as an overlapping winger as a counter offensive threat. In one of my games I intercepted a ball and played it out to the winger and ran down the wing to collect it again.

As I ran down the wing I felt as if I was running in slow motion. It felt effortless and I had a sense of exhilaration and sheer joy from just moving. The next moment I found myself at the other end of the field shouting for the winger, who had cut inside midfield, to pass the ball. Later my coach and other team mates came to me and exclaimed how lightning fast I covered the grounds from my end of the field to the other end. What seemed like an easy, effortless jog down the field to me was actually a brilliant run.

Bad stress, also known as distress, robs us of our ability to cope effectively with the demands of our daily lives by taxing our physical, emotional, intellectual and spiritual resources. Again, using the Olympic athlete example, those who "choke" allow the pressure they feel to win, to get in the way of their performance.

Oftentimes, it is the favourite who loses to an underdog because the underdog did not feel the pressure of the expectations that the favourite felt. It is all about being "cool" under pressure. All peak performers and high achievers have this wonderful ability. An extreme example of "cool" under pressure was the astronauts on Apollo 13 who guided their stricken craft back to earth under life threatening circumstances. The story was dramatized in the movie *Apollo 13*, starring Tom Hanks and is a movie I would heartily recommend for you to see.

To perform at an optimum level there must be a balance between the level of stress and performance. Too much stress can negatively impact performance and too little stress can have the same effect. This is illustrated in the diagram below.

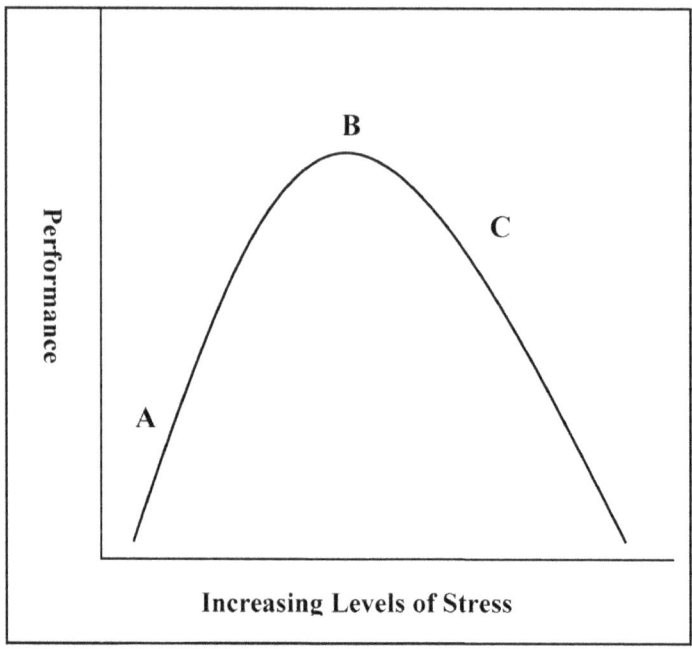

At point 'A' there's too little stress and low performance. At point 'C' the increasing levels of stress have begun to affect performance. The optimum point on the diagram is point 'B.'

Stress and Perception

Your response to stress will be influenced by the stressor and your perception of the stressor. This can be expressed in the formula:

S+P = R or Stressor + Perception = Response [9]

---

[9] Adapted from Jack Canfield's How To Build High Self-Esteem

What is a Stressor?

A stressor is any external or internal stimulation that triggers the stress response. For example, an external stressor can be standing in front of an audience to give a speech. The internal stressor would be the thought that you would appear to be stupid and people would ridicule you. Here both the internal and external stressor reinforces each other, thus trapping you in a vicious cycle.

What is Perception?

Perception can be defined as, "the way we see and understand the events taking place in our environment." Perception can be influenced by our physical senses, personality, culture and gender.

An Exercise in Perception

Study the picture on the next page. What do you see? Can you see the young woman, the old woman and the man? Show the figure to your friends and colleagues. What do they see? What conclusion can you draw from this exercise?

Reflection

1. Based on the definition of stress, what is the most important variable in the equation above?

2. Think of an experience you've had which was influenced by your personality, culture or gender. What was the experience and how did it differ from the experience of others in the same situation?

Reframing Your Experience

Thus far we have said that stress is first and foremost a response to an event and not the event. How we respond to an event depends on our perception or interpretation of that event and that gives us a measure of internal control. The ability to look at a situation or an event in a manner which fosters your ability to cope with that situation in a positive way is called ***reframing***.

It is exercising your power to choose how you look at an event and respond to it. It is choosing to see that the glass is half full instead of half empty. Is there any real difference between a half full and a half empty glass? Not from the perspective of objective reality but from the perspective of subjective interpretation there is a world of difference.

An excellent example of seeing the glass half full was the CBC story of a Calgary man whose house, along with 65,000 other residents of Calgary, was flooded out in June of 2013. The CBC reporter found him with his fishing rod ten feet from his porch fishing. In her interview with him he cheerfully declared that it was not every day the fish came to him and he was going to take advantage of the opportunity. Such an attitude would probably help him to recover more easily from this disaster than many who saw only the negative aspect of the situation.

Reflection

1. Think of an event that you experienced which you labeled as negative. How would you reframe that event to experience it positively?

2. Do you think you would have been able to cope more successfully with this event if you had chosen to experience it from a positive perspective?

Natural Stress Reactions

Whenever we perceive a threat to our survival our natural reaction is to fight or take flight. The fight or flight response is controlled by the old reptilian brain. To get a sense of the structure of the brain make a fist with your right hand, place it in the palm of your left hand and close your fingers around it. The palm of your left hand is the frontal lobe or neo-cortex. It functions as the executive and makes decisions based on logic and reason.

The right fist is the old reptilian brain which controls our survival instincts. The old brain contains the limbic system, which through the hypothalamus, controls the nervous system. The nervous system in turn controls blood pressure, heart rate, digestion. When a threat is perceived, the equivalent of a 911 emergency call is put to the nervous system and there is a red alert. With a red alert, the nervous system dumps adrenaline into the blood stream and the following reactions take place:

- The senses sharpen; the eyes dilate to let in maximum information and light.
- Heart rate and blood pressure increase.
- Breathing and metabolism increase.
- Blood is pumped to the arms and legs; clotting agents are released in the event of an injury.
- The digestive system shuts down and there is a cascade of emotions—anger, fear and fright throughout the system.

These natural reactions have not changed since the time we've been running from sabre toothed tigers and dinosaurs. They are hard-wired into the circuitry of our nervous systems and were appropriate for when we really needed to fight or flee to save our lives. We mobilized our energy and spent it appropriately.

The problem with living in modern society is that we are rarely in a life and death situation, but the same stress reactions are constantly being triggered by trivial issues such as sitting in traffic; waiting in line; being "dissed" by someone or having our belief systems and way of doing things challenged.

The constant triggering of the alarm buttons in our system results in hyper-arousal and eventually wears us down. We suffer **burn-out** and become prone to cancer, heart disease and high blood pressure, a few of the illnesses in which stress plays a part.

These diseases are major killers in North American society and are increasingly so for other cultures which adopt the stress laden North American lifestyle. It is therefore very important to become aware of how we are reacting to a situation and what is happening to us. Awareness lessens the severity of our reactions and hence our proneness to the diseases triggered by stress.

Perhaps the best thing we can do for ourselves is to learn, "not to sweat the small stuff…and it is all small stuff!", as Dr. Richard Carlson asserts in the popular stress management program he developed in the 1990s.

Reflection

1. Recall an event or experience which caused you negative stress or distress.
2. Divide a piece of paper into two columns titled "Physical Effects" and "Emotional Effects." List them.
3. What conclusions can you draw about the physical and emotional effects of stress on you?

A Stress Busting Equation

You can minimize the outcome of a stressful event, certainly from the standpoint of its physical and emotional impact, by the way you react to a stressor. This can be expressed in the following equation as

$$S + R = O \ ^{10}$$

Or

Stressor + Response = Outcome

Another example of reframing one's experience to increase one's ability to cope with a stressful situation is public speaking. It is said that people fear public speaking more than death and is an activity which creates anxiety and "butterflies" in the stomach for most people. Those individuals who interpret their "butterflies" as a sign to run away usually don't do very well and make the situation worse for themselves the next time.

Those who feel the "butterflies" but reframe their experience of nervousness as "excitement" and embrace the opportunity to share this "excitement" with their audience, come across as "enthusiastic" and "inspired."

As these positive experiences accumulate over time, these speakers grow in confidence and skill. It is the same stressor for both sets of individuals, but different responses will have different outcomes.

---

[10] Adapted from Jack Canfield's How To Build High Self-Esteem

The Difference between a Response and a Reaction

We've been using the terms "response" and "reaction" interchangeably in reference to stress. There is however a difference in meaning between the two terms which should be noted. To respond is to consciously take responsibility for our feelings and behaviours. To take responsibility is to take control.

To react is to act in an automatic, "knee-jerk" way to external events and circumstances. With "knee-jerk" reactions, you allow external events and circumstances to determine your feelings and behaviours. This opens you up to feeling like a victim of circumstances with the accompanying feelings of anger and resentment.

The Relaxation Response

The Relaxation Response is the opposite of the stress reaction. It is the ability of the individual to bring the body/mind back into a state of equilibrium and balance by lowering heart rate, breathing, blood pressure and metabolism through a controlled process of breath awareness, proper bodily posture and concentration of the mind.

A Relaxation Response Exercise

This is an exercise you can use to trigger the relaxation response when you are stressed.

- Sit up straight with feet firmly planted on the ground.
- Pull your shoulders up, tense them and let them drop naturally. Let your hands rest naturally in your lap.
- Close your eyes and allow your breath to flow naturally in and out of your nostrils. Do this for a few minutes and become aware of your bodily sensations.

- As you breathe in, experience the breath flowing into your nostrils, into your lungs; experience the rise and fall of your chest and your abdomen.
- With each inhalation, say in your mind, "I am breathing in relaxation and peace." With each exhalation say in your mind, "I am breathing out stress and tension."
- Do this for about five minutes. Record your experience.

Return to this exercise when you experience stress and tension.

Reflection

1. What was it like to just become aware of your breathing and your bodily sensations?
2. How did your body respond as you told yourself to breathe in peace and relaxation?
3. How did your body respond as you told yourself to breathe out stress and tension?
4. Is this an exercise you think will be useful in managing stress and tension? Give reasons for your answer.

The Importance of the Breath

The breath is very important in triggering the Relaxation Response. Humans can survive for weeks without food and several days without water. Without air we die in minutes. Living and breathing are synonymous. The word for "spirit", meaning life force or the power of God and "breath" are the same in many languages.

In Sanskrit it is called *prana*; in Hebrew ***ruach; in*** Greek ***pneuma***. In English to "inhale" is to "inspire" or take in the spirit; to "exhale" is to "expire", to release the spirit.

Proper Breathing and Wellness

Proper breathing is the gateway to physical, mental, emotional and spiritual wellbeing. Most people breathe shallowly from the top of the lungs so carbon dioxide builds up in the cells of the body and brain, resulting in lack of energy and vitality. When the cells are fully oxygenated, energy and vitality flows through the body and heart rate and blood pressure drop.

At the mental level, proper breathing aids in developing concentration and helps to calm and quiet the mind. Slow, rhythmic breathing causes the brain to emit alpha waves, an indication that the body/mind is in a state of relaxation and equilibrium.

At the emotional level, proper breathing interrupts the automatic, reactive stimulus/response reactions, thus replacing anxiety, fear and anger with equilibrium, courage and patience. And at the spiritual level proper breathing integrates body and mind, conscious and unconscious processes.

Breathing from the Core

We've been talking about "proper breathing" and the question is "what is proper breathing?" Proper breathing is breathing from the core. The core is situated just below the navel. To find the core bring your four fingers together and tuck your thumb into your palm. Place the fingers just below the navel. In Zen meditation practice, students are taught to place their attention and awareness in this area as this is a meeting point of physical and spiritual energy.

Breathing from the core is also known as abdominal or diaphragmatic breathing. The diaphragm is the main muscle responsible for breathing. It is a dome shaped muscle located at the base of the rib cage and divides the lungs from the abdomen.

Breathing from the core causes the abdominal muscles and the sides and back of the lower torso to expand outward; the diaphragm lowers and air is drawn into the lungs. The lower the diaphragm drops, the more air is drawn into the lungs.

Breathing from the Core Action Step

- Do this exercise in a place where you can be comfortable.
- Get a book and lie flat on your back.
- Place the book in the area between your navel and pelvis.
- Breathe in, focusing on raising the book with each exhalation.
- Breathe out, and allow the book to fall naturally.
- Do this for 3-5 minutes. Notice how breathing like this makes you feel.
- Practice this technique until it becomes natural to breathe from your diaphragm.

Another exercise which can either be done sitting or lying down is to visualize the bottom of the belly as a balloon. Inhale and see and feel the balloon expand. Exhale and see and feel the balloon contract. Work with this image for a few minutes.

Whenever you catch yourself breathing from the top of your lungs, go back to breathing from your core. Keep a journal on the impact of this type of breathing on how you feel and compare how you feel when you catch yourself not breathing from your core.

Modeling the Power of Water

Another strategy for managing stress is to model the power of water. Water can be a powerful and devastating element, but its "essential nature" is gentle and soft. The Chinese philosophy of Taoism reveres these qualities of water and also because it is adaptable, flexible, and yielding. It flows around, over and under all obstacles and always finds a way out. Taoists recommend that you live and respond to the circumstances of your daily life in the way that water behaves in the natural world.

Managing Change

Change is one of the unavoidable facts of life which contribute to stress. The *I Ching*, an ancient Chinese book of wisdom, describes change as the unchangeable. It is the one constant in everyone's life. One of the most traumatic changes I experienced was being laid off after becoming a new father and getting married. I had always seen myself as an achiever, who was hard working and smart and so when I was laid off I took it very seriously and personally. I interpreted being laid off as a personal rejection of me as an individual and a betrayal by my boss, who, over the course of my employment, commended me on several occasions for contributions I had made at work.

It took me a while to get over the emotional shock and trauma. Part of my process involved taking a thorough inventory of my skills and talents and being open to feedback from family and friends. I was reminded of my excellent writing and speaking skills and the broad interests I had in personal development and peak performance. I also had a solid academic foundation in the social sciences and liberal arts and learned that my interests and academic background could be used in the field of Learning and Development. I ended up working for an international seminar company and found a whole new career path.

Today, I work as a self-employed Training and Development Consultant tapping into all the academic, work and life experience I've gained to help my clients save themselves time, energy and money as they pursue the results they want in their personal and professional lives and businesses.

What I learned from this experience is that "when life gives you lemons, make lemonade" to quote Dale Carnegie. Managing change effectively comes back to attitude. Is the glass half full or is it half empty? My half empty glass perspective, based on fear, defaulted to seeing myself as the victim of the machinations of a hypocritical boss and asked, "Why does this happen to me?" My half full glass perspective, focused on opportunity, asked, "What can I learn from this and where is the opportunity?" Qualitatively different questions give qualitatively different answers.

Since the time I was laid off and now, the world has gone through a cataclysmic recession that has wiped out the economies of countries, decimated industries and devastated the personal lives of hundreds of thousands of individuals and families. There was a time when it was almost commonplace to hear that a father had killed his family and committed suicide because they had lost everything they had worked for.

Such upheavals and changes are predictable and cyclical. The only thing we can do is to be prepared emotionally and psychologically and be engaged in a life-long process of learning and upgrade of our skills. In 1970 Alvin Toffler wrote a book titled *Future Shock*, a term he coined to describe the constant, overlapping, and overwhelming impact of change that is too complex and occurring too rapidly to be easily assimilated by individuals and societies. Future Shock is a condition that is here to stay and is graphically illustrated in the diagram below which shows the escalating volume, complexity and rate of change that contributes to this phenomenon.

Action Step

To get an idea of how much the world has changed, visit with an elderly person and find out from them how the world has changed for them during the course of their lives.

- How has the social, political and economic environment changed?
- What kinds of gadgets and instruments are they using now that weren't around when they were born?
- From this person's perspective, in what ways are the changes better, and in what ways are the changes worse?
- How do you think the world will change in your lifetime? Are you excited by the possibility of these changes, or are you alarmed and frightened?

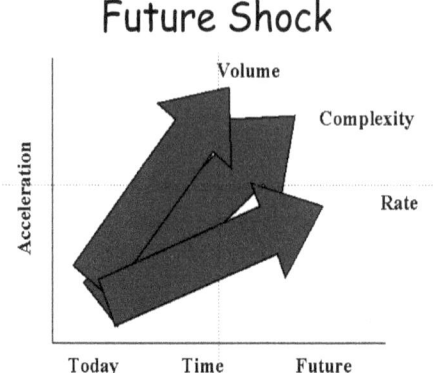

How People Experience Change

The following are some of the ways in which people say they experience change:

- It is difficult.
- It is frustrating.
- It creates discomfort.
- It takes a lot of energy, work and getting used to.
- It causes confusion.
- It is a major challenge.
- It can result in failure.

Some Typical Changes

Here are some changes which can have a major impact on you, your friends and loved ones.

- Death of a loved one.
- Divorce or loss of an important relationship.
- Loss of a job.
- Change in financial status.
- Change of school.
- Change of neighborhood.
- Migration to a new country.
- New sibling.

Reflection

- List the changes that you've been through or changes which have impacted you in the last year.
- Put a check mark beside the ones which have affected you the most.
- How have they affected you?
- How did you cope with them?

The Importance of Resilience

One of the most important qualities you can develop to cope with change and stress is resilience. Resilience is the ability to stretch and recover quickly and easily from situations which cause hardship and stress. A demonstration of resilience is an elastic band. If you stretch it between your fingers and let it go, it snaps back into place.

Resilient people are:

- Positive.
- Focused on the big picture i.e. how larger social forces are impacting them and the best responses they can make.
- Flexible.
- Organized.
- Proactive.

More Stress Busting Strategies

- Plan and Prioritize.
- Pay attention to your stress signals.
- Exercise.
- Get adequate sleep.
- Eat properly.
- Build and sustain supportive relationships.
- Maintain a positive attitude.

The Importance of Balance

It is very important that as the pace of your life quickens and the demands and pressures on you increase, that you remember to focus on maintaining balance in your life. Many people step into the roaring rapids of their adult lives and allow themselves to be taken on a white water ride, never managing to stop and giving themselves an opportunity to pause and refresh themselves.

The ancient Greeks developed the philosophy of the "Golden Mean." The Golden Mean was the middle between the extremes of too much and too little. The ideal person for them was one who had a harmonious balance between the development of body and mind. Extraordinary achievers invariably have a fine balance in the development of their mind and body.

Stress management and wellness experts emphasize the body/mind connection. Your state of mind affects your sense of health and well-being and your physical health affects how you feel emotionally. Worry and anxiety sooner or later show up as headaches, pain in the neck, tightness in the shoulders and cramps in the stomach. Those symptoms are messages pointing out that it's time to take care of yourself.

As you step out to embrace the promises and opportunities of your life, your watchwords ought to be "Balance"; "Moderation"; "Harmony." A useful affirmation for you could be, "I pursue the Golden Mean in all that I do."

Summary

Stress is a fundamental part of life. The only time you won't experience stress is when you're dead! Since you cannot avoid it, the only thing you can do is to use the stress busting tools you've been given to protect yourself from its negative effects.

The challenges, trials and difficulties you face are the exams which life sets to test whether you have what it takes to become a dragon. A true dragon uses those trials and difficulties to develop indomitable will and courage. Those very qualities will enable you to soar above your difficulties with ease and grace.

No matter what the challenges you face, the fact is that you're free to choose how you respond. That is the most hopeful and liberating insight you can take with you as you embark on the adventures of your life.

In Strategy #6 you'll learn how to Develop Effective Communication Skills.

Larry Johanson

STRATEGY #6. DEVELOP EFFECTIVE COMMUNICATION SKILLS

"The single biggest problem in communication is the illusion that it has taken place." George Bernard Shaw

Learning how to communicate effectively is a pre-requisite for achieving success. To achieve success you need to build relationships; work on teams with others and convince people who can help you, to believe in you. You also need to inspire and persuade colleagues, customers, sponsors, and bosses to invest in your ideas, products and services. You will also need to resolve challenging interpersonal conflicts and issues that will inevitably arise in the course of your everyday life.

All of these activities require effective communication skills.

Many people fail at communicating effectively with each other because they assume that speaking the same language as others is communicating. While speaking the same language is a minimum requirement to establish dialogue, to communicate effectively with others, which involves understanding and being understood, is a much more difficult and complex process.

In this strategy we will explore elements of the communication process and give you tools to master each element of that process. More specifically we'll look at how to develop effective interpersonal communication and presentation skills. The topics that will be covered in exploring this strategy are:

- The elements of the communication process.
- The importance of interpersonal communication skills for achieving success.
- Emotional Intelligence.
- The types of 'noise' that interfere with good communication.
- The importance of empathic or active listening and its elements.
- Communicating effectively with people who have different communication styles.
- How to manage conflict.
- How to make effective presentations.

The Fourth 'R'

The emphasis of our formal education system is on what is termed the '3Rs'. These are ungrammatically referred to as Reading, 'Riting, and 'Rithmetic.

However there is a fourth 'R' which is equally important, but for the most part, the system does not place formal emphasis on learning the skills and qualities required to excel at this skill. This fourth 'R' is **relationships.** The assumption seems to be that you can establish good relationship skills by absorbing it automatically from the environment. That is like expecting you to teach yourself the '3Rs'.

What we learn about relationships and how to develop and maintain them comes from our interactions with others—our parents, siblings, friends, colleagues—and what they teach us. Temperament also plays a role in our ability to develop and maintain relationships. Generally, people who are more out-going and gregarious find it easier to make friends than individuals who are shy and withdrawn.

A Requirement of the Fourth 'R'

To build and maintain good relationships requires the ability to understand the personalities, needs and motivations of the people we live and work with, and our willingness to help them get what they want. At the same time, we need to communicate clearly our wants and needs and get their help in getting what we want. This ability to establish win/win relationships with others is referred to as being "people smart" or "emotionally intelligent."

In Strategy #3, we said that being "People Smart" was a gift or talent that came naturally to some people. It can also be a skill that one learns. How does one go about understanding the personalities, needs and motivations of the people one lives and works with? It takes empathy; the willingness to step into someone else's shoes; to look at the world from their perspective and to honour and respect that perspective.

Emotional Intelligence

We also spoke about EQ or Emotional Intelligence as another type of "Smarts." Emotional intelligence (EQ) was defined as one's awareness of one's emotional states, the ability to effectively manage these states, and to help others become aware of, and manage their emotional states. EQ is regarded as perhaps the most important intelligence because it determines the quality of one's relationship with others, and hence one's happiness.

The Traits of People with Emotional Intelligence

People with Emotional Intelligence have the following traits:

- Self-awareness.
- Ability to manage their emotions.
- Self-discipline.
- Empathy.
- Ability to successfully manage relationships with others.

Reflection

- What do you understand by the term "self-awareness?"
- Describe a time when you were angry with someone and managed to keep your cool. What did you do?
- Why would self-discipline be an element of Emotional Intelligence?
- What is the difference between "empathy" and "sympathy?"

The Importance of Communication

Communication is a uniquely human ability. Humans are the only species to use language to convey meaning as we do. Interpersonal communication skills are important to our personal and professional success because they enable us to develop, manage and nurture those personal and professional relationships.

According to Brian Tracy, in *The Psychology of Achievement*, "fifteen percent of our success comes from our technical skills; 85% comes from our ability to deal effectively with other people." The ability to deal effectively with other people is a function of our communication or people skills.

Communication or people skills become more important than your technical skills, especially when you begin advancing in your career and take on leadership roles. In many cases, your technical skills will help you get promoted to a leadership role, but your communication skills become more important because, as a leader, you are expected to get things done through others.

Brilliant but socially awkward people are oftentimes led by people who are not as brilliant but who have communication and people skills.

What is Communication?

The word "Communication" is derived from the Latin *communis* meaning "common." Communication can be defined as the process by which people establish a common understanding between each other by using symbols such as words, pictures and numbers.

The Communication Process

The following diagram illustrates the dynamics of any communication process.

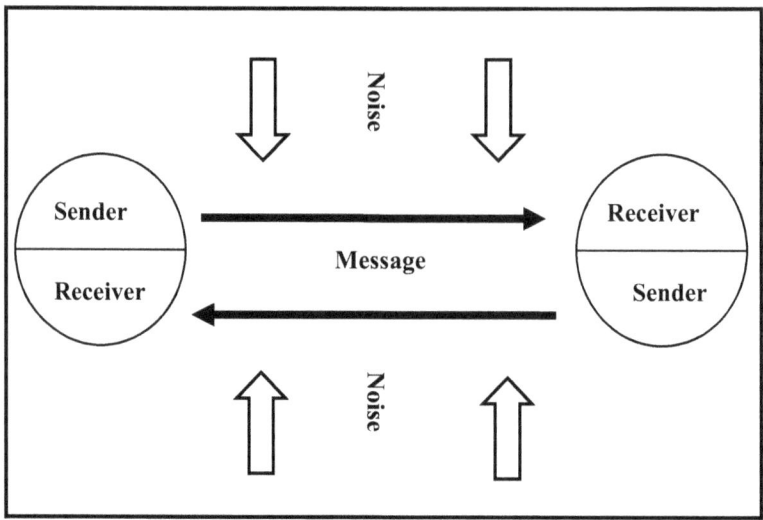

In every communication process there is a source, a message, a receiver and a channel through which the message is communicated. Harold Lasswell, a noted communication scholar, summarized the communication process in the following formula as:

Who says **What** to **Whom** over what **Channel** with what **Effect**

The diagram shows the sender (**Who**) transmitting the message (**What**) to the receiver (**Whom**). Every message is sent with the intention to get a response or effect. As the diagram shows, 'noise' impinges on the communication process at all aspects of the process. Noise can be described as anything which interferes with the sending and reception of a message. Noise can be external or internal.

Types of Communication Noise

There are six types of communication noise that interfere with the transmission of your messages. These are:

Environmental – e.g. the sounds of sirens close by or a blaring radio that prevents you from hearing what is being said.

Mental – e.g. your values and beliefs that clash with the values and beliefs of the other and so both parties fall back into a defensive mode rather than staying open to hear, understand and explore what each other is saying. The other mental noise is the intrusion of your own thoughts even as the other person is communicating to you.

Emotional – e.g. anger and fear. These emotions are huge obstacles in the way of effective communication. They trigger more of a flight/fight response rather than a desire or ability to communicate rationally and logically.

Words and their meanings. Different generations have different meanings for words. When I was growing up, if something was very good it was described as 'bad' by the hip, young people of my generation. The first time I heard a 'Gen Xer' describe someone as 'sick', I thought that the person they were referring to was not well, only to realize that they meant that the person was 'amazing', and confirmed how out of date I had become with that generation as an aging baby boomer.

Social – e.g. bias, prejudice, dislike. We are disinclined to give people an opportunity to share their point of view if we don't like or have a bias against them.

Disorganized message. Awkward expressions and unskillful grammar and punctuation can make it difficult to understand a message.

> **Reflection**
>
> 1. Which of the communication noise listed above do you encounter the most in your communications with others?
> 2. Why do you think you encounter these types of noise in your communication?
> 3. What can you do to lessen the types of noise you encounter?

The Three Modes of Communication

The figure graphically represents the three modes of communication and their relative effectiveness when people are engaged in face-to-face communication.

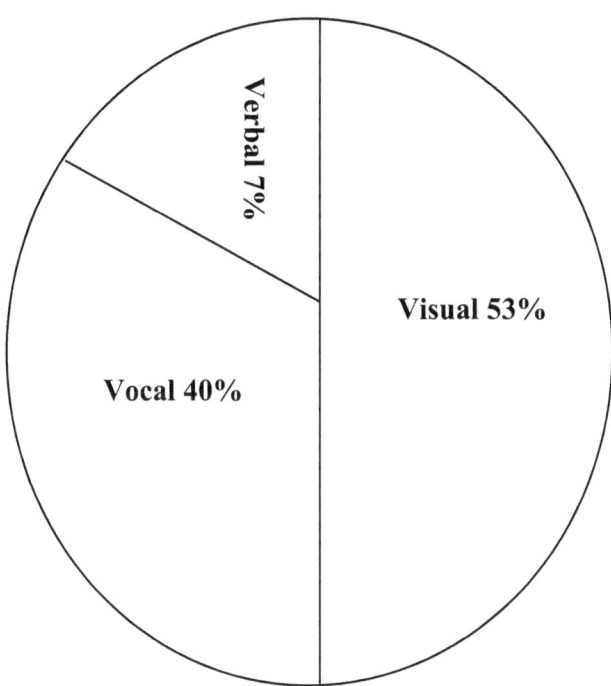

The visual mode includes dress, posture, body language and gestures. People receive more information visually and so even today in the highly mediated communication environment in which we live, communication via video is more effective than audio or written language.

The vocal mode includes inflection, tone, emphasis, pronunciation and speed of speech.

The verbal mode is the actual words we use and is the least effective mode of communication. *How* you say something is more important than *What* you say.

> **Action Steps**
>
> 1. Observe people as they go about their everyday lives, being mindful not to stare or make them uncomfortable. Can you infer how they are feeling or the nature of the relationship they have with the person they are interacting with?
> 2. Partner up with someone and say "You're a great person" to convey that a) they are terrific b) that you mean exactly the opposite of what you say. How was it said on both occasions? Ask your partner to tell you what visual cues if any, accompanied the statements.
> 3. Based on your experience, would you agree about the relative effectiveness of the three modes of communication?

The Importance of First Impressions

A very important aspect of the communications process is the impression you make on a person when you meet them for the first time. As the saying goes, "You never get a second chance to make a first impression." First impressions are important because people judge and are judged on first impressions. First impressions can either open or close doors of opportunity depending on the context you're in.

Making Your Best First Impression

How can you ensure that you make your best first impression all the time? The following are some guidelines.

1. Pay attention to your appearance (clothes, grooming, posture, gestures, and facial expressions).
2. Pay attention to how you sound (voice quality, volume, tone, rate, confidence).
3. Pay attention to what you say (vocabulary, grammar, how informed you are).
4. Listen carefully. It is said that the best conversationalists aren't the people who dominate a conversation with their own views, but the people who listen carefully and make a genuine attempt to understand the other person by asking questions and seeking to clarify their understanding by paraphrasing the person they are communicating with.

Going for a Job Interview

Perhaps the context where making your best first impression matters most is going for a job interview. And it doesn't matter whether you're applying for a job as a baby sitter or for your dream job after college or university. When going for a job interview you need to follow these six guidelines:

1. Wear clean, well pressed clothes and polished shoes. Men should wear a black suit, white shirt and a solid tie. Women should wear a pair of closed medium height shoes or pumps, dark skirt that go just below the knee with a high collar blouse and matching jacket. The overall aim if you are a woman is to appear businesslike and professional.
2. Pay close attention to grooming, especially hair, teeth, finger nails and skin.
3. Know why you want the job and be able to articulate this well.

4. Be able to say how you will bring value to the employer and why you are the best candidate for the job.
5. Listen very carefully to questions and ask the interviewer(s) to repeat or clarify their questions if you don't quite understand what they are asking.
6. Be prepared to give specific examples of times you demonstrated leadership, interpersonal communication, and problem solving skills and initiative to get superior results, as these are the behaviours employers want to know you will demonstrate on the job.

The Importance of Listening

It is said that listening is twice as important as speaking and that's why we have been given two ears and only one mouth. Listening is important also for the following reasons:

1. It is the most frequent type of communication activity.
2. It is ranked as the most important on-the-job communication skill.
3. North American employees spend about 60% of their time listening to others.
4. College students spend about 53% of their time listening.
5. The most frequent complaint by couples in disputes is that their partners don't listen to them.

Steps in the Listening Process

The following are the steps in the listening process:
1. **Hearing**—just the physical act of sound waves reaching the ears.
2. **Attending**—the process of filtering out some messages and focusing on others.
3. **Understanding**—making sense of a message.

4. **Responding**—giving observable feedback to the speaker.
5. **Remembering**—the ability to recall information after hearing it. Research suggests that people forget half what they hear *immediately* after hearing it.

Reflection

Think of and write down instances when:

a). You heard the other person but did not attend to what they said.

b). You heard what they said but forgot it immediately.

c). You attended to, and remembered what was said, but did not understand the message.

d). You understood the message but did not give any indication of your understanding.

e). You failed to remember some or all of an important message.

How did these listening breakdowns affect your relationship with these people at the time when they occurred?

What conclusion can you draw about your listening habits?

What can you do to improve your listening skills?

Empathic Listening

In the process of listening there is a special kind of listening called empathic listening. Empathic listening, also known as active listening, increases the odds of understanding someone. It involves

- Listening to get inside the other person's frame of reference and understand their point of view.
- Listening with your eyes and your heart.
- Paying attention.
- Withholding judgment.
- Allowing the other person to speak without interruption.

Stephen Covey in *The 7 Habits of Highly Effective People*, argues that the greatest compliment you can pay and the best way to validate someone is to listen to them with the sole intention of understanding them.

The following reflection exercise should give you a good sense of the effect of empathic listening on your relationships and your own listening habits.

> **Reflection**
>
> 1. Think of a time when someone paid complete attention to what you had to say and you felt they understood your feelings and point of view completely. What did they do?
> 2. How does it feel when someone listens to you completely? Give reasons for your answer?
> 3. Think of one of your favourite persons. Is that person a good listener and one of the reasons they are one of your favourite persons?
> 4. Describe a time when you listened empathically to a friend who needed support? What did you do? How did your friend respond?
> 5. How does it feel when you are talking to someone and you realize they are not listening to you? How do you know that they are not listening?
> 6. What are your thoughts and actions when you decide to "tune out" someone?

Two Rules to Promote Understanding

The processes described here are designed to promote understanding between yourself and others. Here are two rules to remember.

First, make the effort to understand the other person's point of view before requiring the other person to understand your point of view. Second, in seeking the other person's understanding, do everything you can to help that person to understand you. How can you help others to understand you? Here are six steps.

1. Be clear about what you want to say.
2. Use words that have the same meaning for you and the person you're speaking to.
3. Be honest about your feelings.
4. Match your behaviour with your words.
5. Insist on speaking without interruption.
6. State what you want, not what you don't want.

> **Reflection**
> 1. Why is it important to understand the other person's point of view first?
> 2. What are the challenges involved in trying to understand the other person's point of view first?
> 3. Think of an interpersonal challenge you were faced with in which you tried first to understand the other person's point of view. What did you do and how did it work out?

Understanding Behavioural and Communication Styles[11]

One of the cardinal rules of effective communication is that for it to take place, we have to know who we are communicating with. That is, we need to know who our **audience** is, what makes them tick, what are their needs, their motivations, their values and what's in it for

---

[11] This section on Understanding Behavioural and Communication Styles relies on the work of Dr Tony Alessandra who was gracious enough to grant me permission to use the behavioural style matrix in *The Platinum Rule* which he co-authored with Michael J. O'Connor. *The Platinum Rule*™ is a registered trademark of Dr. Alessandra.

them, if they listen to us and take the actions we recommend or suggest. It is said that if you want to be successful communicating with your audience, then you need to tune in to the radio station **WIIFM**, or "What's In It For Me."

Some of the most gifted and successful communicators in history, Sir Winston Churchill, Martin Luther King Jr., President Kennedy didn't rely solely on their superb ability to weave words with magical and potent effect, but combined that ability with their knowledge of their audience and spoke to the self-interest of that audience.

From the earliest times, philosophers and psychologists have puzzled over the inherent differences in people. What causes one person to behave in a particular way and another to behave completely opposite? They attribute these differences to temperament. Temperament is innate and makes you different from another person in the same way that an apple tree and an orange tree differ from each other. Beneath the differences, there is a basic "treeness" but apple and orange trees are just different. With us there is a common humanity, but there are also obvious differences.

They argue that temperament drives our behaviour and many efforts have been made to categorize and explain the different types of temperament and behaviour. The consensus among the various thinkers, philosophers and psychologists is that there are four types:

1. Some people are forceful, direct, results-oriented
2. Some are adventurous, optimistic, talkative
3. Some are cautious, conservative, responsible
4. Some are precise, accurate, detail-oriented

Some of the most prominent classification systems are DISC; Myers-Briggs; True Colours and Dr. Alessandra's Behavioural Styles. I found Dr. Alessandra's classification relatively simple and easy to grasp, hence my choice.

According to Dr. Alessandra, there are two behavioural styles—Open and Self-contained which contrasts as follows.

Behavioural Styles

Open	Self-Contained
Relationship oriented	Work, task oriented
Express emotions and feelings openly	Guarded
Animated	Keep feelings private
Friendly	Formal and proper
Informal	Little or no facial expressions
Willing to discuss personal issues	Avoid or minimize social contact

OPEN

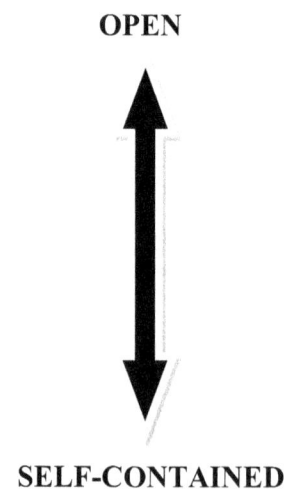

SELF-CONTAINED

> **Reflection**
>
> 1. How would you describe your behavioural style based on these characteristics?
> 2. How would you describe the style of your work colleagues, parents, siblings and friends?

Similarly, the communication styles are either indirect or direct and compare and contrast as follows:

Communication Styles

Indirect	Direct
Slow paced	Fast Paced
Cautious	Risk social encounters
Make qualified statements	Make emphatic statements
Ask questions for clarification	Express opinions readily
Reserve opinions	Intense
Diplomatic	Confrontational

> **Reflection**
>
> 1. Based on the descriptions of "Indirect" and "Direct" Communication styles, how would you describe your communication style?
> 2. How would you describe the style of your work colleagues, parents, siblings and friends?

Personality Types

The combination of behavioural and communication styles give a certain personality profile which Alessandra and O'Connor categorize as follows:

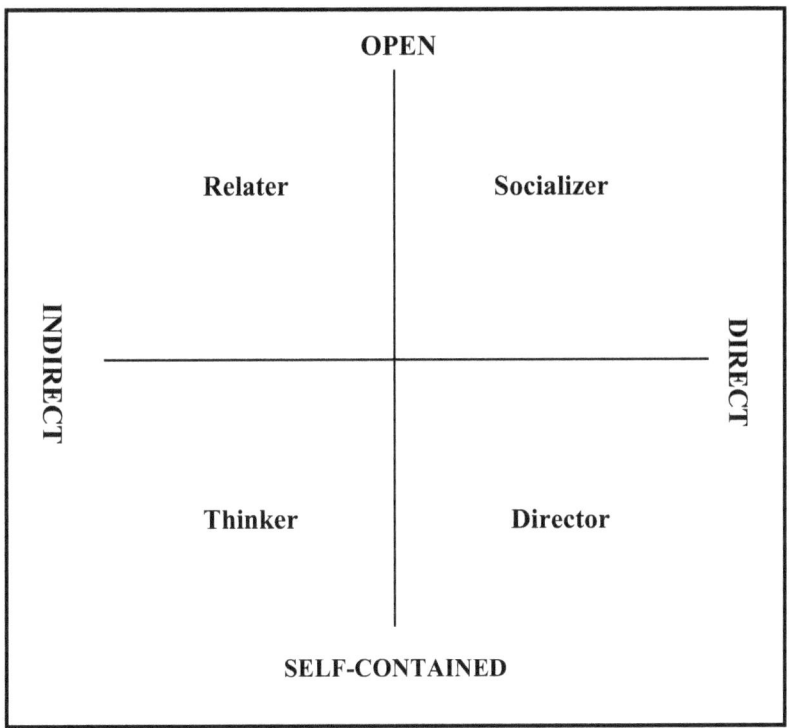

The Behavioural and Communication Style of the Socializer

- Open and direct.
- Expressive, talkative, outgoing.
- Fast-paced; lots of ideas.
- Fun loving; playful, enthusiastic.
- Hates details; lacks follow-through.
- Wants to be liked; craves recognition from peers.
- Can be sarcastic under stress.

The Behavioural and Communication Style of the Director

- Self-contained and direct.
- Dominant; driving; need to be in charge.
- Loves to achieve; overcome obstacles.
- Task oriented; works hard; efficient.
- Can be blunt and insensitive.
- Hates inefficiency and indecision.
- Under stress can become dictatorial.

The Behavioural and Communication Style of the Thinker

- Self-contained and indirect.
- Serious; analytical; logical.
- Cautious; thorough; detail oriented.
- Well organized; accurate; dependable.
- Can be nit-picking; critical and perfectionist.
- Withdraws under stress.
- Hates surprises and unpredictability.

The Behavioural and Communication Style of the Relater

- Open and indirect.
- Friendly; easy-going.
- Moves at a slow and steady pace.
- Pleasant, cooperative team-player.
- Cares deeply about others' feelings.
- Can become submissive under stress.

- Dislikes insensitivity and impatience.

> **Action Steps**
>
> - Review the characteristics of the Personality Types.
> - Choose the one which fits you most closely and give reason why?
> - Using this model, how would you describe the style of your work colleagues, parents, siblings and friends?

The Importance of Understanding Each Other's Style

It is important to understand each other's style; that people relate to each other out of their own needs, motivation and values, which are influenced by their styles. People whose styles are diagonally opposite each other in the matrix run a greater risk of misunderstanding each other because of the greater contrast in their behaviour and outlook.

The open and direct Socializer, who thinks fast, talks fast, loves the big picture and lacks follow-through, would have challenges working with the self-contained and indirect Thinker who is cautious, thorough, detail oriented and a perfectionist. The same is true for the Thinker. The Socializer would probably find the Thinker a "boring, stuck-up person." The Thinker, on the other hand, would probably label the Socializer a "shallow, social butterfly."

Similarly, the self-contained and direct Director, who is results oriented, efficient, driven to achieve and dictate, would have challenges dealing with the open and indirect Relater, who is slow, steady, and cares more about how people feel than about results. The Relater on the other hand, would come away feeling bruised after an encounter with the Director. The Director would probably label the Relater as "needy and sentimental"; and the Relater would label the Director as "abrasive and ill-mannered."

It is important to note that none of us are a pure style. We all possess elements of the other styles to one degree or the other and use them, perhaps unconsciously, when the situation demands. People are described as a particular style only because that style is their dominant style.

Which of these styles is the best? Actually, none is. Each brings its own strengths to the table. We need the results orientation of the Director, the sales and marketing skills of the Socializer, the coordination and team-building skills of the Relater and the planning and attention to details of the Thinker.

The point is that people are naturally and temperamentally different from each other and those who try to understand, adapt to, and work with these differences will end up being in a better position of achieving their goals because they would become more effective communicators.

The Challenge with the Golden Rule

Applying the concept of the Behavioural Styles quickly points up the limitations of the Golden Rule, according to Dr. Alessandra. The Golden Rule and its variations say, "Do unto others as you would have them do unto you." It is embedded in the assumptions and practices of all the great religions of the world and is seen as a formula for establishing and maintaining great relationships because of its implied assumptions of fair play, justice and equality.

However, in a world of increasing diversity and interdependence, and especially in multi-cultural and ethnically diverse societies, living by the Golden Rule may not achieve what it was intended to do. Why? Because the emphasis is on treating people how **you** would like to be treated. This means dealing with people from your perspective. We all have different needs, desires and perspectives. What I want and need may not be what you want and need and so treating people according to my criteria of what is desirable treatment can backfire.

I learned that lesson early in my career as a manager in Jamaica. Jamaican society and social context was, and probably still is strongly authoritarian. People with authority wielded it with no expectation of being challenged and conversely subordinates were expected to fall in and toe the line. It is one of the vestiges of a colonial society where the only acceptable answer to the plantation owner was an unqualified "Yes!" This cultural expectation played itself out in the home where parents wielded absolute authority in the rearing of their children and carried over into the workplace. I chafed under this kind of authoritarian leadership and had difficulty with some bosses I had. I decided that if ever I found myself in a position of authority I would treat people in the way I would want to be treated as a subordinate, which was to be assigned the task and left to get on with it.

When I became a manager in this context I immediately made good on the promise I made to myself. I consulted with people, sought their views, gave them their assignments and left them to use their resources and initiative to complete the tasks without over supervising them. Soon I began to get feedback that some people expected to be told not only what to do, but how to do a task, and that I was seen as shirking my responsibility as a manager. I quickly realized that applying my standards on how I wanted to be treated as a subordinate didn't work for everyone and that I had to be sensitive to the context I was functioning in.

The Platinum Rule™

The way out of this dilemma, according to Dr. Alessandra is the Platinum Rule. The Platinum Rule states "Do unto others as they would like done unto them." The benefits of the Platinum Rule is that an effort is made to understand people from *their perspective*—their needs, desires, motivations. They are treated in a way that they consider is best for them and brings out the best in them. The Platinum Rule is thus a more sensitive version of the Golden Rule.

Action Steps

1. Practice applying the principles of the Platinum Rule.
2. Using the knowledge you have of behavioural styles and the principles of the Platinum Rule, list three things you could do to improve the relationships between you and the significant people in your life.
3. Pay attention to those relationships you have challenges with.
4. Record the improvements in your Journal.

The Principle of Win/Win

Another powerful principle that you can use to govern your relationship with others is the principle of win/win. In a win/win relationship people seek only what is beneficial to everyone in the relationship. They play fair and are respectful of the feelings and wishes of each other. Where there are differences, they cooperate to resolve them in a way that leaves everyone satisfied with the decision.

Stephen Covey in *The 7 Habits of Highly Effective People*, said that his commitment to this principle helped him to facilitate a complex and difficult negotiation where lots of money and prestige were at stake and where one-upmanship characterized the relationship prior to him coming in as a facilitator. By setting that principle as a ground rule for negotiations and by pledging that, "I don't win, if you don't win", he was able to get people to work together as collaborators to resolve their differences rather than as advocates seeking the best advantage of one side.

The test of really effective interpersonal communications is that everyone in the relationship feels valued and safe enough to be open, authentic, natural and spontaneous with each other.

Our Relationships as a Stamp Collection

The interactions between ourselves and others can be compared to collecting and trading stamps. We collect and trade "Friendship" stamps when we treat each other with kindness and sensitivity. We collect and trade "Jerk" stamps when we are unkind and insensitive to each other.

Relationships that flourish and grow collect and trade more "Friendship" stamps than "Jerk" stamps. Relationships that lose goodwill and trust, and thus weaken and die, collect more "Jerk" stamps than "Friendship" stamps.

The aim is to make our stamp collection full of valuable "Friendship" stamps that we can trade in for happiness and peace.

Action Steps

- Divide a page into two columns titled "Friendship Stamps" and "Jerk" stamps.
- Under the "Friendship Stamps" column, list the things you could do to create valuable friendship stamps between yourself and the people you have relationships with.
- Be mindful that you have to treat each according to their temperaments and needs.
- Under the "Jerk Stamps" column, list the things that you have done to weaken the relationship.
- Begin working on increasing the size and value of your "Friendship Stamps" collection.

Managing Conflict

The consequences of poor communication and misunderstandings are conflicts. The whole point of developing effective interpersonal communication skills is to minimize conflicts and focus one's energy and time on achieving one's dreams.

However, if you find yourself in a conflict with someone, and the chances of being in conflict with someone at some point in your life are guaranteed, the following are some steps you can take to resolve the conflict:

- Stay calm; stay centered.

- Breathe deeply.
- Listen carefully; don't interrupt.
- Acknowledge the other person's view point.
- Seek win/win solutions.
- Don't blame.
- Speak in a calm, even tone.
- State your point of view clearly.
- Play fair.
- Honour agreements.

These then are some of the key principles you can apply in establishing and maintaining effective interpersonal relationships. We'll now look at the other key communication skill of effective presentation skills.

Effective Presentation Skills

Achievers have an ease and ability to present their ideas and concepts to their publics in engaging and compelling ways. The people at the top of their fields are invariably masters at public speaking. It is said that speaking in public ranks number one among the top ten human fears as follows:

1. Speaking before a group
2. Heights
3. Insects and bugs
4. Financial problems
5. Deep water
6. Sickness
7. Death
8. Flying
9. Loneliness
10. Dogs

Comedians like to point out that the person who is doing the eulogy at someone's funeral would prefer to be in the casket. Why do people get anxious and stressed when faced with the prospect of speaking in front of a group?

Reasons for Nervousness

People get nervous for a number of reasons. These are:

- Fear of failure
- Fear of ridicule
- Fear of rejection
- Embarrassment or loss of face
- Judgment from the audience
- Imagining the worst

How to Overcome Nervousness

A certain amount of nervousness is desirable. The old advice is to make the 'butterflies' you feel fly in formation. How do you do that?

Prepare.

My motto is "Preparation is Paramount for Powerful Presentations."

Preparation involves:

- Knowing your topic very well, especially the introduction, as you are more inclined to be nervous during the beginning of your presentation.
- Knowing your audience very well.
- Being clear about your purpose. Do you want to inform, educate, or entertain?
- Being clear about the actions you want your audience to take and asking them to do so.

- Being confident that what you're offering is a gift that will shift them into a higher state of consciousness and save them time, energy, and money, improve their relationships or contribute massively to their personal development and effectiveness, and have proof that this is so.

Take care of yourself.

- Be well rested and nourished.
- Dress comfortably and appropriately to enhance your self esteem and self confidence.
- Breathe deeply from your core.
- Take your time. Pause.
- Be familiar and comfortable with the technology you're using, having in place backup systems—computers, batteries, lamps, bulbs, data storage.

Summary

We live in an age where technology and the integration of media have given us unprecedented abilities to communicate and connect with each other. Yet the billions of words we send and receive seem to get in the way of us communicating with each other. Many of us are trapped and isolated on lonely islands of misunderstanding. To avoid the tragedy of too much talk and too little communication we need to use all the tools at our disposal to build bridges of understanding between us. In a world filled with conflicts and strife, one of the greatest contributions you can make to building peace and harmony, is to become a skilled communicator. It is a moral duty of one who wants to awaken, cultivate and transform the dragon in you.

In Strategy #7 you'll learn how to apply what you've learned so far to Develop Entrepreneurial Skills and create wealth.

Larry Johanson

From Carp To Dragon

STRATEGY #7. DEVELOP ENTREPRENEURIAL SKILLS

"The entrepreneur always searches for change, responds to it, and exploits it as an opportunity." Peter Drucker

When I was growing up I never entertained the thought of becoming an entrepreneur or going into business for myself. The path mapped out by my teachers in high school was to go to university and become a professional. I never associated practicing a profession with conducting a business even though that's what professionals do in selling their services. I stumbled into business only after being laid off and going through the humiliation of being considered "unemployed" and the frustration of pounding the pavements looking for a job.

I then took a position as an "independent consultant" with a seminar company, which meant that I had no benefits as an employee and I only got paid when I worked. From there it was a short hop working for myself and through a process of trial and error, losing money and paying huge amounts of money to marketing gurus, some of whom I later learned only gave a partial picture of what it took to run a successful business, did I finally learn how to do it.[12]

---

[12] By far the most comprehensive training and support I've received is from Joel Bauer, mentor and coach to some of the world's most successful marketers and speakers. His Passion2Profit and ProfitPoint deep immersion marketing training are

Business and entrepreneurial skills are crucial for survival in a world of accelerated change and "Future Shock" where industrial society is giving way to a knowledge based economy. As this process unfolds, old industries die even as new ones begin to emerge. Accompanying this are massive shifts in the way economies distribute jobs, resulting in millions of people around the world losing high paying manufacturing jobs and having to retool and acquire new skills to survive in this brave new world.

There is no such thing as job security anymore. The days when one could leave high school and follow one's dad into a manufacturing plant and spend the rest of one's working life in a guaranteed job are over. During the course of one's working life one can expect to have anywhere from three to five new careers. The worker of the future will have to commit him or herself to continuous learning and to be flexible and adaptable enough to change with the times.

The people who have survived and thrived in good and bad times are entrepreneurs because of their ability to see and seize opportunity when others are stymied by problems. Some of the qualities we referred to earlier as qualities that high achievers or dragons possess or cultivate, are the same qualities that entrepreneurs possess and cultivate. It is not surprising that one of the most popular shows on CBC Television featuring some of the most successful entrepreneurs and venture capitalists in Canada is called *Dragon's Den*.

Characteristics of Successful Entrepreneurs

What are the characteristics of successful entrepreneurs? These are:

---

second to none in helping his students get results. Check him out at www.JoelBauer.com.

A clear vision of what they want to accomplish. Successful entrepreneurs have a good sense of what they want to do, what they want to accomplish, when and how. They have clearly written mission statements that they consult on an ongoing basis to determine where they are in relation to their goals.

High self-confidence and self-esteem. Successful entrepreneurs feel good about themselves. They know that they are capable and worthy of achieving great things and don't allow critics in their circle to prevent them from pursuing their dreams.

The ability to take risks and tolerate huge doses of uncertainty. Successful entrepreneurs are calculated risk takers. Everyone who starts their own business undertakes huge personal and financial risks and although all entrepreneurs expect to be successful, there are no absolute guarantees that success will follow. The would-be entrepreneur needs to acknowledge the possibility of failure and still be one hundred percent committed to the success of her enterprise.

The ability to manage stress well. Stress becomes a close companion of entrepreneurs who have to put in long hours and are constantly trolling for new customers, contracts and projects to ensure a steady revenue stream. Successful entrepreneurs are conscious of a balanced and healthy lifestyle and strive to take care of themselves.

The ability to manage time well. Successful entrepreneurs in the early stages of their enterprise wear several hats at the same time. They are the president, the delivery person, the janitor, the customer service representative, the sales person and much more. They have to be able to prioritize and invest in those activities that will bring them the best returns on their investment of time.

Openness to learn, to try something new and not to fear failure. Successful entrepreneurs are creative thinkers and problem solvers, constantly seeking new, more efficient and effective ways of creating value for their customers and themselves. Most people refrain from trying something new because they fear failure more than they desire success. Successful entrepreneurs are driven more by the desire for success than their fear of failure.

Optimistic. Successful entrepreneurs have a positive "can do" attitude. They prefer to see the glass as being half full instead of it being half empty. This ability to reframe their perspective to emphasize the positive gives them the resilience to bounce back from disappointing experiences.

Disciplined. Successful entrepreneurs have the ability to set goals, deadlines, and plans and to stick to them in spite of the temptation to engage in more pleasurable short term pursuits.

Self-motivated. Successful entrepreneurs are driven from within. They set their own challenges rather than allowing external peer and environmental pressures to dictate their actions.

The ability to think creatively and create new opportunities where others see obstacles. Successful entrepreneurs have the ability to bring new perspectives to old problems, to intuit new trends, tastes, and shifts in the market long before others who spend their time resisting change. The result is that they become trend setters and innovators, capitalizing on new opportunities even before others respond.

The ability to build and sustain relationships. Successful entrepreneurs have the ability to build and sustain relationships with customers, creditors, suppliers and others that they have to interact with on an ongoing basis. They genuinely like the people they work with and are themselves easy to get along with.

Assume full responsibility for themselves. Successful entrepreneurs don't blame others for their setbacks and misfortunes. They look first at their own role to see what lessons they can learn and move on.

Successful entrepreneurs acquire these personal characteristics and technical skills by observing other successful entrepreneurs, by asking and paying for good advice, and by reading extensively and committing themselves to a process of lifelong learning. Above all, they are committed to personal excellence and integrity in their personal and business affairs.

The challenges of becoming an entrepreneur are great but the risks are in proportion to the rewards. Becoming an entrepreneur opens you to the exciting possibility of becoming independently wealthy. Most of the millionaires in the world are business owners. A well-off owner operator of a small trucking company told me that he could not work for anyone because he could not stand the thought of having someone determine how much he could earn.

Even if you don't become an entrepreneur it is important to take an entrepreneurial approach to your career—that is, to see yourself as an independent consultant to your company with the mission to increase and add value to it. In that way you step out of the role of being a mere employee and become a partner and co-creator with your employer. As such, you become the President and CEO of 'You Inc.' That mindset will prepare you to create value and opportunity for yourself and others throughout your working life. It will increase your odds of being seen as one of the MVPs (Most Valuable Players/Producers) in your company and hence more likely to keep your job when decisions are being made to let people go when the business environment changes.

Choosing a Business

You may be wondering what business you should go into and again the advice which was given in Strategy #3 about discovering your passion, your gifts and talents and doing what you love, and loving what you do, is true for the type of business you get involved in. Many people turn a hobby or interest into very lucrative businesses. The business gurus advise that the key to choosing a profitable business is to identify a hungry market and give the customers in that market what they want. Better yet is to identify a niche, that is a prequalified group of customers who are hungry for the product or service you are offering and for whom there are few or no satisfactory options.

Network Marketing

A good alternative to starting a business from scratch is to become involved with a network marketing company. No less a luminary in the field of wealth creation than David Bach, author of *Start Late, Finish Rich* recommends getting involved with a network marketing company as a rapid way to build wealth. The advantages of getting involved with a network marketing company according to him are:

1. The company has a product or service and a tried and proven marketing system and tools.
2. Starting is relatively inexpensive.
3. You can gain access to coaching and training from people who are successful in that business and whose continued success is based on developing leaders such as yourself.

4. Your success is based on building and leveraging the collective efforts of the individuals you've sponsored into the organization.

Learn the Fundamentals of Business

To start and operate a successful business you need to have a basic understanding of how to run a business. You need to understand accounting, production and distribution, sales and marketing, income and cash flow statements. For the budding entrepreneur, there are government and community organizations dedicated to helping him or her write a business plan, and even to identify sources of capital and financing. Use all the resources and sources you can tap into to help you in your business.

Achieving Financial Freedom and Success

According to George S. Clayson, author of *The Richest Man in Babylon*, "Money is the medium by which earthly success is measured." An integral aspect of becoming a dragon is gaining a certain measure of financial freedom and success. Each of us probably has a different understanding of what financial freedom and success means. For me, to achieve financial success is to be debt and mortgage free; to have accumulated enough money to fund the lifestyle I would like to have in my retirement, including possibly another 20-25 years of living after the mandatory retirement age of sixty five, and enough left over to contribute to causes and charities I would like to support.

As modest as this definition of financial success is, many people go into their senior years saddled with debts and a mortgage and precious little for their retirement. Many end up relying on government, their relatives or charity to provide them with the necessities of life. Financial stress can have a devastating impact on the quality of one's life and one's relationships and this is why we'll focus now on some of the key principles on how to make, keep and grow one's money.

What is Wealth?

Before I started to investigate and pay attention to how people become wealthy, I thought of wealth as the physical assets one had; the amount of money one had in the bank, one's home, the land, the buildings one had as part of one's portfolio. As my research took me deeper into the subject of wealth and how people become wealthy, I came across a startling revelation. The physical assets that we typically count as wealth are merely the manifestation of a more fundamental aspect of wealth, and that is that wealth is an attitude of mind, an orientation to the world.

The creation of wealth begins in the invisible realms of the Mind and Spirit. These realms are not limited by anything in the visible world but are themselves the architect of the visible world. They are the *original substance* or *formless stuff* which form the raw material out of which all things come, according to Wallace D. Wattles, author of *The Science of Getting Rich*. Because we all possess minds and spirits, which are unlimited in their creative potential and capacity to create, we already possess everything we need to create wealth and abundance in life. To gain access to this unlimited realm of creative and abundant possibilities we need to change our thinking and challenge our limiting beliefs.

According to Bob Proctor, author of *You Were Born Rich* and contributor to *The Secret*, the international bestselling manifesto on how to achieve abundance and prosperity,

"You must begin to understand that the present state of your bank account, your sales, your health, your social life, your position at work, etc., is nothing more than the physical manifestation of your previous thinking. If you sincerely wish to change or improve your results in your physical world, you must change your thoughts and you must change them immediately...You were "Born Rich" and your abundance is contained in thought. So be good to yourself, choose magnificent ideas, and cease permitting your physical world to control your thinking." (p. 22)

Napoleon Hill, author of the seminal work *Think and Grow Rich*, and whose ideas inspired and continue to inspire generations of men and women who seek wealth and abundance, argues similarly that, "thoughts are things, and powerful things at that, when they are mixed with definiteness of purpose, persistence, and a burning desire for their translation into riches, or other material objects." (p.19)

Winning the Inner Game of Achieving Financial Success

The strategies that we've already discussed as strategies that can be applied to becoming an achiever can be applied specifically to achieving financial success. We have to win the inner game of achievement before our success is manifested in the outer world, and winning the inner game is conceiving and believing that what we want to accomplish is within our powers to do. To win the inner game is to overcome whatever doubts and fears we have and banish the notion of "I can't."

If the realm of Mind and Spirit is a realm of unlimited potential, then in order to harness this unlimited potential, we have to be able to tap into this realm. How do we do this? We do this through the power of zazen (meditation), affirmations and visualizations. In Strategy #2, where cultivating the dragon's mindset was explored, you received a step by step process of creating powerful affirmations and visualizations in order to develop high self-esteem and self-confidence.

To become financially successful one has to feel worthy of being wealthy and capable of achieving it. So the first step is to affirm that you are worthy and capable of achieving wealth and abundance.

The affirmation may go thus: "I am worthy and capable of achieving wealth and abundance. Yes I am! Yes I can!"

Do this in front of a mirror and invest the phrase with energy and conviction. Feel the power, the energy, the joy and anticipation of realizing this affirmation. Let it become a mantra, repeating it constantly until you have no doubt that you are worthy and capable of achieving wealth and abundance.

To increase the potency and power of the affirmation, link it to a visualization of what wealth and abundance means to you. How much do you have in your bank account? What would you be doing, what would you have if you achieved your financial goals? Using all your senses, what would you see, smell, taste, touch if you achieved your financial goals? Revel in the sense of satisfaction and accomplishment that would accompany this achievement.

In Strategy #3, Finding Your Mission and Purpose, you received a process for creating a Vision Board that reflects the ideal life you would like to live. You could have your Vision Board reflect the pictures of your financial achievements—the house you want to live in, the car you want to drive, the places you want to travel to, the experiences you give yourself and your family.

What are your limiting beliefs about Money?

T. Harv Eker, author of the *Secrets of the Millionaire Mind* and creator of the transformational three day *Millionaire Mind Intensive* Workshop, argues that the challenges and difficulties people have about money are directly related to their limiting beliefs about it. He maintains that we all have a money blueprint—an internal model of our financial success.

This prompted me to examine this for myself; to look at my own beliefs and blueprint that I have about money, as I too struggled with growing and maintaining wealth. I quickly discovered that one of the limiting beliefs I had, which was passed down from my mother, was that rich people would never get to heaven and that the price of entry to heaven was suffering, poverty and deprivation here on earth. She was always fond of quoting Jesus' admonition that it was easier for a camel to pass through the eye of a needle than for a rich man to enter the Kingdom of Heaven.

In its essence, this key limiting belief went thus: "To be rich is to risk going to hell!" What a powerful limiting belief! After all, who wants to go to hell? My mother lived this injunction thoroughly and ended up for most of her life struggling and in need while she pined after the sweet hereafter. The interesting thing about my mother was that her father was a wealthy man who was known as "Mr. Money Bags" but who died a lonely and bitter man, suspicious that everyone around him was only after his money. And the land that her mother left, to be divided among her and her siblings, prompted fights that threatened bloodshed.

Her solution was to abandon and relinquish all claims to the wealth that she was entitled to and to embrace the hope of a heavenly reward. She passed her limiting beliefs about money on to her children based on the bitterness of her own experiences with mean and greedy relatives. We need therefore to examine our limiting beliefs, the context out of which they come and to let them go. So what are your limiting beliefs about money and wealth?

Here are a few that I have come across:

1. To get rich I have to do something bad or dishonest.

2. If I get rich people won't like me for who I am but for my money.
3. I am not worthy enough or good enough to be rich.
4. Most of the good opportunities are gone.
5. The only ways I can be rich is to inherit it or to win the lottery.
6. Money is the root of all evil.
7. I don't know anything about money.
8. I am too young to get rich.
9. I am too old to get rich.
10. I am not educated enough to get rich.

You could come up with as many limiting beliefs about money as there are people on the planet.

Reflection

Take a moment to reflect on *your* limiting beliefs about money. What are they? Write them in your Journal.

Take each of your limiting belief about money and turn it into an affirmation.

For example, the very popular limiting belief that money is the root of all evil could be turned around thus: "Money allows me to do a great deal of good in the world."

How much Money do you want?

It is not enough to just want to be wealthy. In Strategy #4, I talked about the importance of setting SMART goals—that is goals that are specific, measurable, attainable, realistic, and time bound. This same principle applies in the case of achieving financial success. How much will your net worth be? When will you achieve this? How much will you earn next year? What financial habits will you begin to develop now to achieve your financial goals?

It is important to note that in setting your financial goals, the little voice inside of you will get loud and hysterical, telling you that you are crazy; that you'll never achieve that goal and try to convince you that it is unrealistic to set such a goal. You'll probably get more resistance from setting this goal than any other goal because of the limiting beliefs you have about money and your ability to earn what you want. This is the time to employ the technique T. Harv Eker recommends when the volume of the little voice goes up. The technique is to say to the little voice, "Thank you for sharing!" and go right on affirming that you will earn the amount of money you want at the specified time and most importantly, take action.

Action Steps

1. Determine the amount of money you want to make and by when.
2. Write it down as an affirmation. E.g. I will have a net worth of (x) amount by (date).
3. I will earn at least (x) amount next year.
4. I will (do what) to become debt free by (date) starting now.
5. To help you in this process engage the services of a financial advisor and have them help you map out a process of becoming financially independent and what you need to do to achieve this.

Principles of Wealth Creation

Ideally, everyone who has marketable skills and has spent 25 to 30 years employed in a job or career that pays them enough to take care of the bills and have some thrills should go into their retirement years with a certain amount of financial security. Yet the sad fact is that many of us face retirement saddled with debt and an old age circumscribed by lack. This condition could be avoided if all of us at the beginning of our working life put a plan in place for creating wealth. The problem is that most of us become consumers rather than investors, procrastinators rather than action takers.

Before we know it we find ourselves facing a bleak future in what really should be our golden years. So what can those of us who have some time on our side do to ensure that our golden years are just that? Here are some principles of wealth creation that we can follow:

1. **Pay yourself first.**

    This principle works to ingrain the habit of saving in us. Most of us pay everyone but ourselves first. The aim is to save 10% of your income and invest it so that the money works for you, instead of you working for it.

    - The idea is to create multiple streams of passive income through your investment strategy.
    - To accomplish this, you will need the services of a professional financial planner with impeccable credentials. Choosing a financial planner is a lot like choosing a doctor or lawyer. Get recommendations from people you trust and who are knowledgeable in this matter. A criterion for accepting their advice is that they themselves are financially secure.

2. **Budget.**

Many people have no idea what is their income and expenditure. The cardinal rule is not to spend more than you earn. T. Harv Eker has designed a system which he argues is the easiest and most effective way to manage one's money and which allows you to save, invest and splurge, all at the same time. He suggests that you separate your income into 6 different accounts, each for a specific purpose. These are:

   i. **Necessity (NEC) Account**—50-55%. This account covers rent/mortgage; food, shelter, clothing. If your necessities take up more than this amount you need to either increase your income or cut back on expenditure in this category.
   ii. **Financial Freedom (FFA) Account**—10%. This is never spent and is used for investment. This is the account for your retirement income.
   iii. **Long Term Savings for Spending (LTSS) Account**—10%. This is for big ticket items such as a car. If you're in debt, then 5% of the money in this account goes toward debt servicing.
   iv. **Education (EDUC) Account**—10 %. This is as important as the FFA Account. You need to constantly upgrade your skills to stay current in a knowledge driven economy.
   v. **Play Account**—10%. This account is for you to splurge on yourself! The one requirement is that you blow it on yourself in any way you choose. You are also to spend it monthly or quarterly.
   vi. **Give**—This varies between 5% and 10% depending on what you choose. People use this account as their tithing account.

The genius of T. Harv's system is that embedded in it are very sound wealth creation principles and in following this system you will end up building assets instead of accumulating liabilities. You can literally eat your cake and have it too!

Summary

In the introduction I noted that the dragon in Chinese culture symbolized power, prosperity and good fortune and represented the imperial power of the emperors. In today's world the people who embody this aspect of the dragon archetype are the enlightened entrepreneurs who amass great wealth, power and influence and use their assets as philanthropists to open doors of opportunity and relieve the suffering of others.

Oprah Winfrey, Bill Gates, and Richard Branson are examples of entrepreneurs who have used their vast wealth in this manner.

The strategies, tools, tips and techniques I've shared with you can transform you into a successful, enlightened entrepreneur. These are the kind of entrepreneurs we need to bring their creativity and energy to solving the monumental problems that confront the planet. Psychologists have found that the happiest, most fulfilled individuals are those who share their good fortune with others.

Accumulating wealth with this intent is a noble pursuit. It should help you eradicate the limiting beliefs you have about money. May you be truly healthy, wealthy, wise and happy.

CONCLUSION

These then are the seven strategies that will awaken, cultivate and transform the dragon you. To recap they are:

1. Lay a foundation of right character.
2. Cultivate the dragon's mindset.
3. Find your mission and purpose.
4. Manage and invest your time wisely.
5. Breathe your stress away.
6. Develop effective communication skills.
7. Develop entrepreneurial skills.

If you've made it to this point, done the reflection exercises, and taken the recommended action steps, then you ought to congratulate yourself. You will have come a long way in creating and designing the life you want. You will indeed become the master of your destiny by making the choices that will increase your chances of living a life of health, wealth, wisdom and happiness. What I've shared with you is the best advice and mentoring I can offer grounded in my real life experience and the application of the strategies I discovered, summarized and packaged for you in simple, digestible, bite sized chunks.

You will also save yourself considerable time, energy, and money. But you must act. My experience tells me however that it is the rare individual who has the determination and persistence to take action even if the steps are clearly outlined. I offer a coaching program that offers a system of accountability and support that will help you overcome the obstacles you encounter on the way to transforming the dragon in you.

If you need support in taking the steps that I've recommended, then visit my website at www.CarpToDragonCoaching.com and sign up for my coaching program. I'll always be there to support you and cheer you on to achieve the success you deserve. You can also order copies of the book for someone whom you think could benefit from reading it. There are discounts for ordering 10 or more copies.

I love, absolutely adore receiving feedback. If you benefitted from reading the book and implemented the strategies let me know how this program has enriched your life. Send your testimonials, either video or written, to ljohansonC2D@gmail.com.

I close with the inspiring words of Marianne Williamson, author of *A Return To Love,* words it is said that inspired Nelson Mandela as he led his people in the long march to freedom.

>Our deepest fear is not that we are inadequate.
>
>Our deepest fear is that we are powerful beyond measure.
>It is our light, not our darkness that frightens us.
>
>We ask ourselves, who am I to be brilliant, gorgeous, talented and fabulous?
>
>Actually, who are we not to be?
>
>You are a child of God.
>
>Your playing small doesn't serve the world.

From Carp To Dragon

There's nothing enlightened about shrinking so that
other people won't feel insecure around you.

We were born to make manifest the glory of God
that is within us. It's not just in some of us, it's in everyone.

And as we let our own light shine, we unconsciously
give other people permission to do the same.

As we are liberated from our own fears,
our presence automatically liberates others.

That's a very poetic and beautiful way to say that when you awaken, cultivate and transform the dragon in you, you awaken, cultivate and transform the dragon in others. What a wonderful journey to embark on!

Larry Johanson

SOURCES

Alessandra, Tony. Ph.D., Michael J. O'Connor Ph.D. *The Platinum Rule.* Warner Books, 1996.

Bach, David. *Start Late, Finish Rich.* Double Day Canada, 2005.

Canfield, Jack. *How To Build High Self-Esteem*, Nightingale/Conant, n.d

Clason, George S. *The Richest Man in Babylon.* Signet Books, 1988

Covey, Stephen R. *The 7 Habits of Highly Effective People.* Simon and Schuster, 1990.

Eker, T. Harv. *Secrets of the Millionaire Mind.* Collins, 2005.

Franklin, Benjamin. *The Autobiography of Benjamin Franklin.* Houghton Mifflin Company, 1923.

Hill, Napoleon. *Think and Grow Rich.* New York: Fawcett Columbine, 1937.

Kapleau, Philip. *The Three Pillars of Zen.* Anchor Press, 1980.

Powell, Wallace D Wattles & Dr. Judith. *The Science of Getting Rich.* Top of the Mountain Publishing, 1993.

Proctor, Bob. *You Were Born Rich.* Life Success Productions, 1997.

Salzberg, Sharon. *Loving-Kindness: The Revolutionary Art of Happiness.* Shambala, 1997.

Toffler, Alvin. *Future Shock.* Random House, 1970.

Tracy, Brian. *The Psychology of Achievement*. Nightingale/Conant, n.d.

About the Author

Larry Johanson is an author, speaker, life coach and corporate trainer on Personal Development, Leadership, Communication and Change Management. He is a lifelong practitioner of Zen meditation and an explorer of the farther reaches of human growth and potential. His simple mission is to be a conduit of light and joy to every girl and boy, no matter their age, wherever they are in the world, and in whatever context they live.

Contact Larry Johanson at 1-800-571-0635 to enquire about his coaching programs, seminars and workshops. Visit his website at www.CarpToDragonCoaching.com.

www.ingramcontent.com/pod-product-compliance
Lightning Source LLC
Chambersburg PA
CBHW060521090426
42735CB00011B/2320